The Money Diet

Biblical Prescriptions for Financial Success

Richard T. Case, M.B.A.
Paul Meier, M.D.
Frank Minirth, M.D.

BAKER BOOK HOUSE

Grand Rapids, Michigan 49506

Unless otherwise indicated, all Scripture verses are from the Holy Bible,
New International Version, copyright 1973, 1978, International Bible
Society. Verses marked KJV are from the King James Version.

Contents

Introduction

I had been in Dallas about two years when I met a young man who seemed unusually wise for his age. His name was Richard Case. As I recall that meeting, Job 32:7-9 goes flashing past my mind: "I thought, 'Age should speak; advanced years should teach wisdom.' But it is the spirit in a man, the breath of the Almighty that gives him understanding. It is not only the old who are wise, not only the aged who understand what is right." Here was a man who, although young in years, was not young in wisdom. The Almighty, indeed, had given him understanding.

I had been around one Christian friend who is very giving. I had been around another Christian friend who was very saving. I had another friend who had no debt. I had Christian friends who took good care of their families. Some spent wisely. But I had never known personally any man who seemed to have all of these abilities. My first impression of Richard was that perhaps he was such a man. I never shall forget the words he spoke in a sermon years ago: "Money is a small thing. It is a test. If you can be faithful with money, then you can be faithful with a larger ministry God has for you." The words hit home. Was I such a man?

I finished my medical training about two years prior to meeting Richard. As a medical student, I had been in poverty. But I had been out for approximately two years and was working hard. If I had known the principles of this book I would have definitely changed my approach to managing our money. As I got to know Rich and applied these principles, my financial situation improved greatly. To be honest, I must still wrestle with certain questions: What is really important in life? What is God's view of money? Have I been praying about financial matters? Am I getting wise counsel? Am I monitoring current investments? Am I spending too much? Am I confusing wants with needs? How is my sales resistance? Am I giving what I should to the Lord? Do I have a savings plan for times of crisis? Do I have debt? Am I spending wisely?

These are questions I wrestle with, and I am sure the reader does also. I would encourage the reader to ask the same questions and then to apply these principles. Six months from now the improvement may be impressive. In this book, Richard answers these questions through the use of Scriptures and God's leading in his own life. (Richard, too, isn't perfect!) And frankly, though I wish he or none of us would ever fail, I am glad God has led Richard through certain trials so that I can identify with him and benefit by his wealth of knowledge.

Well, Richard, I agree — "Money is a small thing." However, the management of it may hold the key to our ministry.

Frank B. Minirth, M.D.

CHAPTER ONE

Money

Say that one word — *money* — in a large crowd and you will arouse a wide variety of emotions:

Some will have *joy* at the expectation of getting some money.

Some will have *grief* as they remember having recently lost some money.

Some will have *anger* and *bitterness* as they are reminded of their financial setbacks.

Some will have *guilt* for having so much money when they don't feel as if they deserve it.

Some will have *jealousy* because they think, if they can't be rich, no one else should be either!

Some will have *self-righteous pride*, because they assume all their wealth is the result of being God's favored child.

Others will have *self-righteous pride* because they have chosen poverty and have given away all their wealth to charitable causes, so that they can subtly brag about it.

There are more verses in the Bible on money than on heaven and hell. There are scores and scores of verses that tell of financial and other blessings for those who are living for God. At the same time, the Bible tells us that money is the root of all sorts of evil. Seventy percent of marital conflicts are over money (usually power struggles over how to spend it). Some of the godliest men in the Bible were also the richest men on planet Earth: Abraham, Isaac, Jacob, David, Solomon,

Job, Joseph (of the Old Testament), Joseph (of the New Testament, who supplied his tomb for Jesus' body), and others. Others were like the Apostle Paul. He experienced periods of time when he "abounded" and periods of time when he was "abased" and poverty stricken. Jesus made His twelve disciples carry no money at all when they traveled toward Jerusalem with Him. Later, when He was about to experience His death and resurrection, He told them to carry some.

A Little Bit More

As a Christian psychiatrist, I have counseled hundreds of people on financial matters. As a human being with faults of my own, I have experienced a wide variety of blessings and humiliations over money matters myself. I have lost thousands of dollars of financial investments that were bad deals. Some were offered by fellow Christians who I was foolish enough to believe. I also have experienced materialistic cravings. My wife and I have a little sign in our bedroom that says "All I want in life is a little bit more than I will ever have!" This is to remind us of the stupid attitude that all of us depraved humans tend to have.

One of the best decisions I ever made was the decision to move to Dallas to begin a full-time ministry with Dr. Frank Minirth in 1976. At the time, I was a professor of pastoral counseling at Trinity Seminary in Chicago, a school I still admire and love. A short time before, I had been given an opportunity to give up my seminary ministry for a high-paying psychiatric job, running a clinic. In fact, because of my materialistic urges, I had decided to make that job change at the end of the school year.

Seek Ye First . . .

But then Paul Little died. He was a professor at Trinity and a very dedicated man of God. I went to his funeral, where Leighton Ford preached the funeral sermon. He spoke on the importance of being able to look back on your life some day and realize that you were a pioneer for Christ, like Paul Little had been. I was deeply convicted and fought off the tears. I knew at that moment that God wanted me to turn down that job opportunity and instead accept an offer to teach full-time at Dallas Theological Seminary. The verse in Matthew 6:33 (KJV) came clearly to my mind.

But seek ye first the kingdom of God, and his righteousness; and all these things shall be added unto you.

It hurt to give up the financial security I was turning down, but I felt a real peace about my decision. My wife was actually relieved when she heard what I had decided. She had been convicted in a similar way.

I came to Dallas in 1976 and helped pioneer some counseling courses with Dr. Frank Minirth at Dallas Seminary. Since that day at Paul Little's funeral, I have written over fifteen books to use in our classes. Our clinic has grown to become the largest Christian psychiatric clinic in the world. We have around thirty Christian psychiatrists, psychologists, and counselors working for us, all of whom are dedicated to Jesus Christ. We treat missionaries from all over the world at reduced rates (or free in some cases) to get them back on their feet emotionally.

I came to Dallas to pursue ministry, expecting to live a very simple life financially. But, because of book royalties, investments with Rich Case, etc., my income has become much more than it ever would have been had I taken the high-income job back in 1976. I am able to live well and yet give a large portion of our clinic profits to help Christian works throughout the world. Now we are starting the Dallas Graduate School of Psychology, to train future Christian psychologists to meet the severe shortage of Christian psychologists throughout the world.

Purchasing False Significance

Let me share with you a very important insight I have gained into *money* since 1976. I have learned this insight through a combination of Scripture meditation, psychiatric research, counseling experiences, and personal struggles, both emotionally and spiritually. This insight is really quite simple.

According to the Book of Ecclesiastes (and many other passages of Scripture, as well), all humans struggle to feel significant. We are all "chasing after the wind." In Ecclesiastes 4:4, Solomon made the following wise observation:

And I saw that all labor and all achievement spring from man's envy of his neighbor. This too is meaningless, a chasing after the wind.

Psychiatric research also shows us that all humans have at least some struggles with inferiority feelings. We feel somewhat insignificant, so we go through life competing with the Joneses in a vain attempt to prove our significance. To do this, we waste our time seeking various *things*, rather than seeking first the Kingdom of God and His righteousness, and then trusting God to *give* us the things we need after we quit *pursuing* them.

Satan's Three Tricks

I have also learned that there are three main "ways of the world" that Satan uses to trick us into pursuing significance. They are described in 1 John 2:16-17 (KJV) as being:

1) *Lust of the flesh* (which includes sexual fantasies, pornography, sexual affairs, eating disorders, etc.). People do *not* have an affair because they "fall in love" with someone else's mate. They have an affair simply because they feel inferior; and competing for the attention of someone else's mate makes a person feel temporarily significant. This, however, is followed by guilt, then by depression, then by suicidal ideation, and the realization that they have played the fool (see Proverbs 5). Lust of the flesh *does not work!*

2) *Lust of the eyes*. This is the one that relates the most to *money*. Lust of the eyes is the desire to buy everything in sight. It is materialism. It is the pursuit of material things in order to feel significant. When John D. Rockefeller was alive and the richest man on planet Earth (before he

became a Christian), a newspaper reporter once asked him, "Mr. Rockefeller, how much money will it take to make you feel significant?" Mr. Rockefeller grinned, thought a moment, scratched his chin, and then wisely replied, "Just a little bit more."In short, *lust of the eyes does not work!*

3) *The pride of life* involves all sorts of struggles to feel significant through power or prestige. This can be a power struggle to dominate a mate, to dominate a church or organization, to dominate a business in an unhealthy way, to dominate through political clout, or even to dominate through wealth and/or prestige.

Again, it is vital to remember that no matter how much *sexual prowess*, or *money*, or *power* you have, *you will still feel insignificant on a deep inner level of consciousness!!*

Finding True Significance

There is only *one way* to really feel significant. None of Satan's tricks work. That *one way* can be summarized as follows:

1) Trust Jesus Christ as your Savior. Tell Him right now that you are depending on His death on the cross and resurrection to pay the penalty for your sins. You are trusting His shed blood to give you eternal life.

2) Dedicate your life right now to Jesus Christ and His Kingdom. Make Him the Lord of your life. Give up the rat race that all of us human beings so foolishly pursue. Give up all your vain and foolish attempts to prove your significance through lust of the flesh, lust of the eyes, and

pride of life. Decide right now to seek first the spiritual Kingdom of God and to seek to attain more of His righteousness (right behavior and attitudes).

If you quit pursuing *things* (sex, money, and power), then God will bless you in unique ways with such things as:

a. A better sex life with your mate to replace sinful fantasies and behavior.

b. Material blessings of various sorts, which you can use to help others *and* enjoy yourself.

c. Opportunities to use your creative *leadership* in various ways to benefit others, to replace dominating others to compensate for your own insecurities. You will find yourself delegating more and dominating less.

3) Realize that your significance comes from your *position* of being in Christ and your *service* for Christ. God declares us to be significant, so believe Him. *You are significant*. You are God's child, God's chosen people, God's ambassadors, the object of God's love. He died for you. Psalm 139 tells us we were molded in our mother's womb according to His plan, and that He thinks about us *individually, each day*, so many times that His thoughts toward us outnumber the sands by the sea.

After expounding on the ignorance and foolish strivings of all of us humans, Solomon concludes Ecclesiastes with the following instruction: "Fear God and keep His commandments: for this is the whole duty of man. For God will bring every deed into judgment, including every hidden thing, whether it is good or evil'' (Eccles. 12:13-14).

4) Don't *live* for money, but go ahead and use the handling of money as a testing ground to see if you are living for God or are still locked into the stupid rat race that all of us tend to fall for. Study *The Money Diet* to develop a balanced perspective on earning, saving, giving, and investing. Enjoy the money God gives you. Enjoy the emotional and spiritual blessing God gives you as well. Remember that Christ Himself told us in John 10:10: ''I have come that they might have life, and that they might have it more abundantly.''

Paul D. Meier, M.D.

CHAPTER TWO

God's View of Things

One of the most difficult areas for most Christians to deal with is this whole area of having things — materialism, money, and success. We ask ourselves the question, "Should I have more or should I be poor? Should I give all my money away and live like a pauper? How should I handle the fact that God is blessing me but that I have guilt? God says we are not supposed to be of the world, so shouldn't we repudiate all of these material things? In terms of our accumulation and management of things, it seems as if it would be easier either to have so much that we didn't have to worry about it, or to have nothing."

God Gives Us Money

Many people ask me, "What is God's view of money?" "Does He want us to have it or not?" A simple answer is yes! We are required in life to participate with material things. We need clothes, we need shelter, we need jobs to obtain money so that we can buy the things that we need. Since money is required of us, we must learn to deal with it.

God's view of material things, I believe, is a very healthy one. In the Garden of Eden, God looked around and showed Adam and Eve everything that they had — beauty, utensils for hoeing, a till to till the ground, and a command to bring it under their subjection. He actually asked them to *work*, and that was prior to the Fall. In

Deuteronomy, God promised the Israelites that they would conquer a land that would be flowing with milk and honey. They would never have any need for welfare lines because, if they followed His principles, He would guarantee their material satisfaction, which means freedom of worry from financial matters. He said, "I will give you houses. I will give you crops that will flourish. I will give you vineyards that will flourish. The key is just to keep your dedication to me and not to violate my scriptural principles."

So God *gives* us things, but He doesn't want us to be *controlled* by them. He says very clearly that we cannot serve mammon (money) and God at the same time. It is impossible to keep seeking money, which includes worrying about it, and to serve God at the same time. Our mental energy just won't allow that.

He also tells us to seek His kingdom and His righteousness and all these things will be added unto us. This means that He wants us to focus on Him and His principles, rather than on the accumulation of things. He also tells us that things are fleeting, that life is but a vapor. He tells us that if we lay up treasures on earth, dust and moth will corrupt them and, when we die, we won't take any of them with us. Instead, we are to lay up treasures in heaven, such as faith and belief in His Word.

Money Management—Spiritual Faithfulness

So God has provided things for our enjoyment, and I believe that our perspective on *things* is a *demonstration of our stewardship and faithfulness in spiritual matters*. If we are incapable of managing our everyday finances, which are a part of each of our lives, whether rich or poor, I believe that God may not trust us with spiritual things either. He says very clearly that he who is faithful in little things shall be given great responsibilities.

In Luke, Chapter 16:1-15, Jesus expressed a parable of the shrewd manager. Starting with verse 1, Luke says:

Jesus told his disciples:
"There was a rich man whose manager was accused of wasting his possessions. So he called him in and asked him, 'What is this I hear about you? Give an account of your management, because you cannot be manager any longer.'

"The manager said to himself, 'What shall I do now? My master is taking away my job. I'm not strong enough to dig, and I'm ashamed to beg — I know what I'll do so that, when I lose my job here, people will welcome me into their houses.'

"So he called in each one of his master's debtors. He asked the first, 'How much do you owe my master?'"

" 'Eight hundred gallons of olive oil,' he replied.

"The manager told him, 'Take your bill, sit down quickly, and make it four hundred.'

"Then he asked the second, 'And how much do you owe?'

"'A thousand bushels of wheat,' he replied.

"He told him,'Take your bill and make it eight hundred.'

"The master commended the dishonest manager because he had acted shrewdly. For the people of this world are more shrewd in dealing with their own kind than are the people of the light. I tell you, use worldly wealth to gain friends for yourselves, so that when it is gone, you will be welcomed into eternal dwellings.

"Whoever can be trusted with very little can also be trusted with much, and whoever is dishonest with very little will also be dishonest with much. So if you have not been trustworthy in handling worldly wealth, who will trust you with true riches? And if you have not been trustworthy with someone else's property, who will give you property of your own?

"No servant can serve two masters. Either he will hate the one and love the other, or he will be devoted to the one and despise the other. You cannot serve both God and Money."

The Pharisees, who loved money, heard all this and were sneering at Jesus. He said to them, "You are the ones who justify yourselves in the eyes of men, but God knows your hearts. What is highly valued among men is detestable in God's sight."

Jesus' Teaching About Money

What does Jesus tell us about money?

One, *money is a little thing.* The Scriptures say very clearly that the use of wealth is considered to be a little thing, not an insignificant thing but an important small thing.

Two, *faithfulness in little things (money) is an indicator of faithfulness in big things or true riches (spiritual things).* This is where a lot of us get confused, because we tend to spiritualize money away and falsely assume that it is not important. Those of us who do this falsely assume that it is God's sole responsibility to take care of us, while we are responsible only for spiritual matters.

Three, *we cannot serve both God and money at the same time.* Then, is it possible to serve God, since we have to deal with money? If we are faithful stewards over our money, aren't we serving money and serving God? It seems very confusing. The key is this. God wants us to put money in proper perspective, which is that *money is a small thing.* Money is not the most important thing in our lives. If we will manage it properly and continue to focus on God's principles, we will have financial success and be entrusted with true spiritual riches. God is saying that if we follow principles that He specifies for us in His Word, then we are serving Him.

What *is* serving God? Nothing more than obeying what He wants us to do. So serving God is like a servant who does what the master or boss wants. Is this to say that the employee or servant is never concerned with his or her personal welfare or with taking care of responsibilities on his own? Twenty-four hours a day is he always worshiping the boss? No! Rather, the servant is obeying the principles or parameters that the boss or master has established and demonstrates stewardship over those things for which the master or boss has placed the servant responsible.

That is what God has done with money. He has given it to us and said that we need to demonstrate stewardship over this area of living and that, if we do, we will be promoted. We will then be given blessings, freedom, and more responsibility for things that are much more important than temporal financial matters.

Four, *money is not true riches.* God does not want us to concentrate on accumulating things, because *things* do not bring happiness. *Things* do not go with us when we go to heaven to be with Him forever. *Things* do not represent the most important values in life. Whether we are wealthy, middle class, or poor, we are still able to have the true riches of fellowship with Christ—joy, freedom, and peace in our lives. This is what *true* success is. *Money* is not true riches, but it is a means of operating in the world and of enjoying true riches. It boils down to this: If we are in bondage to money, we have a very difficult time enjoying the true riches God wants us to have.

Five, *money is to be used wisely and faithfully.* God clearly says that it is as important to manage our money as it is to be spiritual. By managing our money properly, we *are* spiritual, and we demonstrate to the world that we will not be caught up by accumulating *things.* We will not be caught up in producing *bondage* for our families and "keeping up with the Joneses" because we have to have more. But rather, we will have the proper perspective on money and, in the process, we will enjoy the other values of life more. God urges us to be prudent in our use of money and to enjoy it, but not to let it control us.

Finally, and this is one of the most important points, *it is possible to be in bondage to money*. Probably, we all can say "Amen!" to that! We can let money *control* us so that we constantly think and worry about it. We fear that the future is not going to be good for us and that we will lose what we have. We worry about the possibility of going into bankruptcy or that we will be embarrassed if the loan company calls us some day and really causes us problems. We are in fear of our current situation. We can be in bondage almost to the point where we can think of nothing else. It is a constant source of conflict and irritation to our family. We go to bed at night worrying about it. God does not want us to be in bondage to money.

God Owns It—We Manage It

Let's explore for a minute why it is so important for us to demonstrate wisdom and prudence in dealing with money.

One, *God is the owner of all things that we have.* He created all things (Gen. 1:1, Rev. 4:11). He says, in Haggai 2:8, that silver and gold are His. In Psalm 24:1, He says the earth is His.

In Deuteronomy 8:18, He gives us the power

to make wealth. He gives us all the good things that we have (James 1:17, 1 Tim. 6:17-19), and only by Him can we have wealth (Prov. 10:22). By the way, He includes something very interesting in Proverbs 10:22: He will not add sorrow or trouble to wealth! So, if we are demonstrating faithfulness, God will bless us and will do it in such a way that He will not add sorrow to it.

What would be sorrowful? It would be sorrowful if we would move away from a close relationship to the Lord. He doesn't want us to have so much wealth that we forget that He is the owner and provider of all things. Neither does He want us to be in such destitution that we are struggling and striving and have no time to concentrate on the Lord.

Two, *we are the stewards of all that God owns.* A steward is defined as one who manages another's resources. Since we do not own material things, only God does, we are simply managers or stewards. We are responsible for the care of these resources. In the parable of the talents, we learn, first, that He entrusts to us within our own ability. God knows exactly what our capacity of managing is and what kind of capacity we have in managing money. He entrusts us only with that which we can truly manage. Second, He has a right to the resources He gives us. Third, He expects dividends and returns on those resources.

Three, *He wants us to invest.* He wants us to utilize His money wisely, according to our ability, and He expects a return on it. This return that He wants involves, first, giving back to Him (as we will explore later) for His purposes of spreading the Gospel to make disciples of men and women. Second, utilizing money wisely represents to the world what it means to have a positive and fruitful relationship with the Lord. These are the kinds of dividends that He expects. He expects us (in Luke 16:10-14) to be faithful, prudent, and wise stewards of all that He has given us, particularly in the way we make transactions involving money.

God's Purposes for Stewardship

God has His stewardship purposes working through our use of finances, whether it be much or little. He does this for the following reasons:

1) *He wants to illustrate His power* (Prov. 3:9-10). He says that our barns and vats will be full if we give a portion of our income to Him. He wants to demonstrate to us and our families what it means to trust God for our financial condition.

It is exciting when, with our families, we sit down and pray for various items and then see God bless us with a gift or with a special arrangement. The children can see directly that it was not anything that we did, but that it was God's hand, because we have been faithful in our stewardship. This says to the children that God cares about them. He can and does manage material things and this really illustrates His power. According to 2 Corinthians 9:13, our use of money glorifies God to both Christians and non-Christians. As we are giving, as we are sharing, as we are coming to the need of other people with our abilities and our financial resources, this says to the world that money is not as important as people. This glorifies God because this is exactly what His value system says.

2) *He wants to provide for all of our needs* (Phil. 4:19). He wants to be the source of our gains, and He wants to be the source of our needs. He loves us so much that every time something good happens to us, He wants us to be reminded of Him and how good He is. The fact is, we can look to *Him* to provide our needs, rather than struggling and striving ourselves.

3) *He wants to unite Christians* (2 Cor. 8:14, 15). Paul asked the different churches to contribute for the need in Jerusalem. Oftentimes, the use of money can bring us unity, through a special program in our church, a special need like the earthquakes in Guatemala, or the droughts in Africa. He wants us to be the providers and to bring ourselves together to focus on the needs of the world. I believe He has a special purpose for America in this regard.

Dr. Paul Meier and I went to Amsterdam, Holland, with the Billy Graham conference for itinerant evangelists in 1983. We were impressed with the great needs of evangelists around the world. The major source of providing funds for these people comes from America. Most Third World evangelists were living on less than fifty American dollars *per month*. God wants American Christians to unite and provide the world with the resources necessary to present the Gospel and have people come to know the Lord. I believe this could be a unifying factor for American Christians.

4) *He wants to confirm our direction in life.* He uses money to demonstrate whether or not He wants us to go forward with a certain plan or not. If we don't have the resources, He doesn't want us to proceed. Jesus said, "The fool is the one who doesn't count up the cost before he embarks on a program."

When Linda and I went to seminary we had two little girls, Christina, four, and Michelle, two. We assumed that if God wanted me to go to seminary, He would somehow provide enough resources for me to go without Linda working, since it was more important for our children to have their mother at home than it was for me to go to seminary. Otherwise, I would not go. We used this to have Him confirm His direction in our lives at that time.

5) *God also wants us to be productive.* He wants us to work. Paul says very clearly, "He who doesn't work, doesn't eat." God does not want us to be idle. God knew that work gives us a feeling of self-worth, accomplishment, being necessary in the world, occupying our minds, and dealing with the everyday issues of life in a positive way. Ask anyone who has been laid off or who has had the privilege of not having to go to work, and you will see that he becomes bored without some activity to keep him moving. Work keeps us moving forward. God uses the whole mechanism of money in providing for our family needs to motivate us to work. The benefits come in terms of our spiritual and psychological well-being.

6) *God wants us to be givers so He can out-*

give us. He wants us to be moving in a direction where we are freely giving of our resources to meet the needs of those around us, the needs of the church, and the needs of the worldwide ministry so that God will be glorified and His people's needs will be met.

CHAPTER THREE

Our Weight Problem

God wants us to have things. He doesn't want us to be controlled by things. He wants us to enjoy them. He wants us to manage them prudently. Then, why do we have such a weight problem? I am sure nearly all of us have overeaten on weekends, or have gained some weight, and our pants have begun to feel a little tight. We go to bed feeling stuffed, uncomfortable, and anxious. We feel bad about ourselves.

This is also what being overweight in the area of *money* does. Our financial situation just doesn't seem to fit us. We are always overburdened with needing more. We seem to be overweight in our financial needs. It is such a burden to us that it produces anxiety. Over 70 percent of marital conflicts involve *finances*. They are not necessarily the central issue, but finances are usually the surface *focus of conflict*. The problem, particularly in our culture, is that we want just a little bit more, particularly lately. We have been caught up in a very materialistic society where having *things* is a demonstration of our *significance* or our *success*.

Wealth is our demonstration to the world that we are important. Unfortunately, even many Christians believe that if we are spiritual we will almost certainly be financially wealthy. Our wealth erroneously becomes the measure of our spirituality. The problem is that no matter how much we accumulate, we still have those feelings of inferiority, and we quickly find out that money does not bring happiness. I have a joke about this. My dad used to tell me that "money cannot buy happiness, but it sure helps you look for it in a lot more places!"

So what exactly is our financial *weight problem*? It is usually one of several things. First, we may have so many loans and so much debt that we can't possibly pay back what we owe. We cannot pay our regular loans every month, so we are under tremendous burden. We either have made a bad investment, or we have borrowed too much money to buy certain things and our income is not up to our expenditures.

Second, we may continue to try to accumulate things through credit cards. We eventually find that our credit card bills accumulate to the point that it is hard to even keep up with regular interest payments.

Third, we may have moved into a bigger house and found that the mortgage and the expenses related to that house have really strapped us. We are making it okay, but we are not able to go on vacation anymore. We are not able to go out to dinner as often. We are not able to entertain with other families as often. As a result, we are beginning to get bored and unhappy.

Fourth, we may be struggling with survival. We have made a big change. We have gone from a salaried position to a commission schedule. We have gone from a corporation to our own firm. We have gone back to school, or we have gone into full-time Christian work. Our expenditures have not come down like our incomes have. We are experiencing difficulty.

Fifth, we may be very wealthy, but with that wealth, we have forgotten that self discipline is still required. We still spend like crazy. We buy boats, second homes. We travel around the world using our credit cards freely. We know we have lots of money coming in every month. We are not saving any. We can't seem to keep ahead. We worry as much about our debts as anyone else.

Sixth, we may have a regular job and a decent income, but we try to make more. So we invest in things that don't work out, or we buy an extra store, or we put our wives into a business of their own. We may find that acquiring more money is occupying all of our time. It requires time after work to try to pay attention to these investments. It consumes our time. Striving after money pulls us under.

Which one of these situations is indicative of you? Are you in bondage? Are you so overweight with financial burdens that you feel uncomfortable? Are you having difficulty managing money? Is it really managing you? The rest of this book will explain, no matter what your income level, no matter what your situation, how you can follow a set of biblical money-diet principles that will bring you financial *success*. These principles *may or may not* bring you great wealth. That is God's decision. But, if applied to your life, they will *certainly* bring you *financial success* and *freedom from financial bondage.*

CHAPTER FOUR

Principle 1: Ask for Help

Have you come to the conclusion that you have a financial weight problem? Then you really must get on the money diet, and you had better get going!

Have you thought about asking God first? "Oh, yes, we pray every day about that," may be your reply. But are you really bringing this before God, sincerely asking for his help? In today's society we are bombarded with self-help messages. How to improve your self-image. How to get over anger. How to make a will. How to be happy. How to become a millionaire. We are conditioned to doing things for ourselves, so we don't usually think seriously about praying for our financial problems.

I know that you probably have read and heard many expositions on prayer, the effectiveness of prayer, how to pray, etc. But take a moment and sincerely meditate on the following verses: "Therefore I tell you, whatever you ask for in prayer, believe that you have received it, and it will be yours" (Mark 11:24). "Dear friends, if our hearts do not condemn us, we have confidence before God and receive from him anything we ask, because we obey his commands and do what pleases him" (1 John 3:21, 22). Read these again. Think on them. God *will* answer your prayers.

As you go on this money diet, what should you be praying about? Really, there are only two ways to solve your weight problem. Number one: increase your income; or number two: decrease your expenses. Pray that God will give you creative opportunity to increase your income and the courage to decrease your spending. Prayer is a means of effecting a partnership relationship with our Lord to accomplish His purposes. What is His purpose for us regarding money? *To be financially free!*

Thus, as we move out on faith, we take certain actions while we expect God to answer our earnest prayers. Colossians 1:29 says: "... I labor, struggling with all his [Christ's] energy...." There is an interesting story that appeared in *Reader's Digest* recently about a man who was in a flood and had moved to the second story of his house. The waters were rising and along came a man with a row boat. The man said, "Get in, we will take you to safety." He said, "No, I'm waiting for God to rescue me." The waters kept getting higher. He got up on the roof. Then along came a man with a speed boat. A voice said, "Get in, we'll take you to safety." He said, "No, I'm praying that God is going to rescue me." And then, finally, the waters were rising almost to the top of the roof and he had to move to the peak. A helicopter came along. A voice said, "Come on, get in. Climb up and we will take you to safety." The man said, "No, I've been praying and I expect God to save me."

The waters kept rising and the man drowned. He went up to heaven, went before the

Lord and said, "Lord, what happened? I prayed and prayed and prayed and I believed you were going to rescue me." The Lord said, "Well, what did you expect, I sent you two boats and a helicopter!"

This story illustrates that we have the responsibility to respond to God's provisions for us.

Increasing Your Income

What is our responsibility for increasing our income? *Diligent labor* (Rom. 12:11). We need to consider the following. Work harder; work longer; knock on more doors; make one more call; do the best you can; possibly change jobs. If your children are in school, maybe your wife could go to work.

In our consulting business, I was given a contact in San Antonio with a man who owns a conglomerate. I had attempted to call him several times and we just kept missing each other. I assumed that he just wasn't interested. I never try to badger clients or potential clients, so I was going to give up.

But I thought about this issue of making one more call, so I prayed to God and said, "I'm just going to make one more call and if you want me to have this contact, it will be there and we will set up an appointment. If not, then I will forget it and move on." I made that one more call and he was in. He agreed to meet with me and he became one of our biggest clients.

If you are in a salaried position, you may not have much opportunity to greatly increase your income. You may want to consider changing jobs where you can get in another company or another industry where your income could increase. If you are on a commission basis, you perhaps need to knock on more doors, work longer, get assistance in leads, develop a marketing campaign, or other such things that would increase your chances of getting sales.

We recently produced a movie on evangelism. I asked one of the actors if he had enough work. He stated that he needed to go on eight to ten auditions before he would be cast. So every week that he had free time, he scheduled a minimum of eight to ten auditions. This is a usual ratio, also, when one owns a business or when on commission. We need to knock on more doors. Proverbs 28:19-20 says prosperity comes from hard work.

The Five Don'ts

However, there are five key things that you should *not* do: First, don't just impulsively step out in faith and do something drastic, such as starting your own business. You may find that God isn't a magic genie that provides instant success. Also it may not be God's will for you to do this. The expenses and the time required to start any business are substantial. If you are already in financial difficulty, you will only get into more difficulty.

Second, don't ever quit your job until you have a better one secured. You may think "Well, since I don't have enough income here I'll just quit and I know God will give me another job." For many people, finding a new job takes a long time. Prudently, you can get out your resumés, go ahead and have interviews after hours and during lunch, and wait for God to provide you with that job if he wants you to change.

Third, don't assume that changing to a commission job will always be the best move. You may think, "Well, my salary isn't enough, so if I can go on commission I know God will bless me." There are many companies that promise a lot but deliver very little, so be careful about going on commission. Also commission work must suit your personality: it's hard work! And, you may encounter many people who say no. Can you handle that?

Fourth, don't fall for any "get rich quick" schemes. I personally have never seen a get rich quick scheme work. As a matter of fact, the Bible says in Proverbs 28:22: "A stingy man is eager to get rich and is unaware that poverty awaits him."

Even the people who seem to have gotten rich quick, overnight, usually haven't. The people who started Apple Computers, for example, spent six or seven years developing the product and living on meager salaries. We only heard about Apple when their stock price zoomed, so we assumed they were lucky and got rich quick. The people who spent all those years struggling knew better. In Proverbs, the Lord says that diligent labor will produce good profits. So beware of any "get rich quick" scheme. It just doesn't work and it will usually get you deeper in trouble.

Fifth, Do *not* borrow money to invest money. You may think, "Well, I'll just invest in this one deal and if it goes well, then I'll be out of hock and I'll be in great shape!" God does not desire that we jeopardize ourselves that way. He wants us to invest money that we are earning above and beyond what we need to take care of our basic needs. So don't get yourself in trouble by borrowing money to invest.

One thing we *can* do to increase our income is to have creative resourcefulness in developing ideas that may produce income for us, even if it is just a scant bit more. Another extra three or four hundred dollars a month might mean a great deal toward obtaining financial freedom. Wives might be able to take part-time jobs or full-time jobs if they don't have responsibilities at home with the children. Learning new skills like computer technology or word processing might be a worthwhile investment, since these are jobs in high demand. Even if it is only on a part-time basis, the income could be enough to put you over your financial hump.

Perhaps you own a company and have a stable product, but have not thought about new markets into which to take the product. There may be a new opportunity that could generate more sales and income for you. You may have hobbies that you excel in which could result in profits. You may be able to turn your creative talent into resourceful income. Maybe there are things you can make at home. Review some of the many magazines now that promote products that you could make at home.

Another of our responsibilities is to watch closely those investments we currently have.

Perhaps we have stocks, bonds, real estate, or other investments that we could now sell to get ourselves out of debt. The key to success with investments is to seek wise counsel. Proverbs 15:22 says: "Plans fail for lack of counsel, but with many advisers they succeed."

Get Expert Help

Most of us are not experts in investing money. A lot of things that look good on paper really are not. So you should rely on competent expert help that understands the markets well and can give you good, sound, well-informed advice.

My wife and I were working our way out of debt after we had learned these principles. We had stock that was given to us by the company that I worked for at the time. I sought competent advice from a professional financial adviser. He told me to hold on to it because he felt that the stock was going to increase significantly over the next year. In fact, it did. It increased three times the value it was at the time I was considering selling it. Then, this competent adviser told me to sell it. I did and made enough profit to nearly clean up the rest of my debt. So, I believe God honored my prayer for increased income by having me seek wise counsel.

Decreasing Your Spending

After we have looked at increasing our income, the next thing we need to look at is decreasing our spending. The first thing we should do is analyze our current situation. The best way to do this is to go through our checkbook and record all of our expenditures in three columns: (1) "must haves," (2) "should haves," (3) "like to haves." "Must haves" include such things as housing, food, shelter, automobile, utilities, insurances, and taxes. "Should haves" include such things as clothes, furniture, etc. All the rest are "like to haves."

The key is to review every item and begin to cut back, starting with the "like to haves" and then moving to the "should haves." Look at your take home net income and pull back your expenditures to at least equal that level, so that your spending is *below* what you are making.

This is no different than that of a firm. When Chrysler was taken over by Lee Iacocca, the firm was approaching bankruptcy. Iacocca did this simple analysis for his firm. He asked his management team, "What are the things we must have, what are the things we should have, and what are the things we would like to have?" He cut out all the things he would like to have, reduced the "should haves" and stuck basically to what they *must* have to be successful. Within two years of "suffering," so to speak, on the part of employees and management, who all took pay cuts, their firm was out of bankruptcy. It has paid back much of its debt and now is becoming a dynamic, progressive transportation company again.

One key element in this process is that of suffering. None of us likes to suffer. Rather, we enjoy living the good life that we have come to be accustomed to in America. Very few of us are willing to sacrifice any of those things, even for a short term, because it is painful. But, it is important to note that, as we go through this suffering, if we are willing to discipline ourselves, God will reward us with the financial freedom that He promises. I can tell you from experience that having the financial burden off is much more exciting than all the things that we could buy or enjoy by staying in debt.

Another key ingredient is not to incur any more debt. Do not buy any more items on credit. It may be important to even tear up the credit cards if you can't handle it so that your out-go always is less than your income. We get drawn into a false sense of security by using credit. We think that we will be able to pay it back later, over a period of time. Then all of a sudden, our payments keep increasing and increasing and we never pay off those debts. So never use any more debt to buy things. Stick to the budget and pay cash. And for those needs that you have, this is where trusting God in faith is required.

When my wife, Linda, and I decided not to use debt anymore, we needed a coat for our daughter, Christina. I was tempted to establish credit at a store and purchase the coat for her, because we thought she really needed it. My wife reminded me that we had agreed not to use credit, and that we would rather trust God and stick to His principles. So, we prayed that God would provide a coat for Christina.

Within two weeks a friend of ours brought over boxes of clothes that their kids had outgrown and said, "I've been thinking that maybe you could use some of this stuff. Why don't you go through this and see if there is anything that you can use, and I'll take the rest to someone else.'' In that box were two fine coats for Christina. God provided for us and we didn't have to borrow.

God really enjoys providing our needs and wants. He wants us to learn to trust Him. We can't do it if we take things into our own hands and use credit cards, when it is beyond our means to use them.

Guidelines for Severe Cases

There are some other guidelines that may seem severe. However, they may be necessary if you are really in trouble and it doesn't look like you have much of a chance to increase your income. You may need to sell that big home that you've moved up to and scale down somewhat. That home can be draining you. You may be really strapped, and every month you have to make those big payments and those big utility bills and it is really causing anxiety. One couple recently discussed this with me, and I encouraged them to sell their house (which had tripled their payment and had become too much for them). They decided to do so and to scale down. You wouldn't believe the freedom and joy that they experienced by reducing their financial burden.

Nothing — no house, no car, no materialism — is going to provide satisfaction. It is going to be the *pressure* that is off our backs that is going to give us satisfaction with our family. We may need to sell some of those extra things that we have accumulated: a second home, a car, or maybe some investments that we have made in real estate or stock. God would much rather have us be in financial freedom than to have things and be under financial bondage. Later, we can prudently develop a financial plan that will enable us to own those things again. But this time, we can own them without the financial bondage going along with it.

If you are in the lower income bracket, you can also look for subsidies that the government provides. HUD provides housing allowances and special home mortgage rates. If you are a veteran, you can get special home mortgage rates. You may be able to have special lunch money subsidized for your children or to receive food stamps. Senior citizens can get special discounts.

By reducing your expenditures, you will experience some suffering. You may not be able to go out to eat as much. You may not get to enjoy as much entertainment. You may have to cancel some trips. You may even get somewhat bored and depressed. However, you will learn to make your own entertainment and do free things. There are parks and museums to visit with your family, lakes and beaches to go to. You can take short trips in one day and visit various places together. You can enjoy playing games with friends in your own home. Maybe God wants you to slow down all your activities and take time to learn to enjoy and love each other better. Many Christian families are so busy with so many things that they are fractured. Perhaps this will be a time when God will really solidify your family by bringing you closer together.

As we do our part, God will then do His part. Perhaps he will allow us to sell that extra thing we have for a good profit. Or, all of a sudden, we will get increases in pay. Or He may provide us with that other job we need. He may open up something for a spouse. But most of all, God wants us to get out of *bondage*. He is not going to bless us until we are disciplined in handling financial matters. God wants to provide us with the things that will bring us happiness. He also wants us to learn to trust Him. So work together with God and ask Him to help you and work hand in hand with Him in going on this financial diet in order to gain *financial freedom*.

Psychiatric Comment:

Just as individuals in the body of Christ have different spiritual gifts that aid in different ministries, so also individuals have different personalities that aid in different aspects of "the money diet." Also, certain personalities will find specific aspects of "the money diet" especially hard for them. Some can give with ease; others find it difficult. Some find that saving is second nature; others just can't seem to save at all. Some have never known debt; others have never known anything but debt. Some spend wisely; others don't. Some enjoy life; others never have. The one who excels in one area may fail miserably in another. Few excel naturally in all areas.

The individual who has a lot of *obsessive-compulsive* personality traits, who desires to control himself and others, may have more trouble asking for help. This individual is perfectionistic, orderly, hard working, dutiful, meticulous, and intellectual. With all those good traits, one might ask why this individual wouldn't ask for help. He may have trouble, because he struggles with insecurity deep within and compensates by being in control. He manifests his problem through pride and is therefore hesitant to ask for help.

Also, the more *paranoid* (hypersensitive, suspicious, jealous, negative, angry, skeptical, mistrustful, loner) an individual is, the less likely he is to ask for help. He may ask God for help, in a sense, but his self-righteous attitude keeps him from personal insight and the resulting changes that he may need to make.

The individual with *hysterical* traits (emotional, excitable, likable, outgoing, dramatic), on the other hand, has no trouble asking for help. However, hysterics' lack of depth and lack of being in touch with deep emotions makes them doubt, deep within, that God really cares for them. Even though they ask, they often do no more. They have trouble carrying through.

The *passive-aggressive* individual (prone to procrastination, forgetfulness, and stubbornness) will ask but then subconsciously find a way to fail. He has internalized anger that he deals with through self-destructive behavior. He asks, only to fight any positive results.

The *narcissistic* individual (who is preoccupied with self, has problems with criticism, and has interpersonal problems because of exploiting others) will ask for help, but for selfish reasons.

As I shared this chapter with my wife, she said we had all of these personality traits, so there was probably no hope for us. We laughed as we realized that her statement was true. All of us have all of the personality traits, but often they balance one another out and, despite their drawbacks, they also have strong points. Also, God is in the business of working with imperfect people. Only when a trait becomes extreme, hindering us greatly in one area of our lives, do we need to be concerned about it.

If you have any of these negative traits that may affect your asking God or others for help, then following the money diet may be your key to overcoming these traits. If your problem with asking is severe, you may need to seek professional psychological help. Don't let problems with asking ruin your opportunity to be financially free.

CHAPTER FIVE

Principle 2: Give First

Contrary to most diets, our first priority in the money diet is to give away that which we are trying to conserve. Most diets suggest that you conserve and cut back. In normal society, we think that we should get ourselves straightened out, then we will be in a position to give money away. Or, we think that, when we become wealthy, we will give some of it away. In the meantime, we need to pay our own bills, because we certainly won't make it if we start giving away our money.

We Give to Receive

A dichotomy of God's principles of living is that instead of saving, instead of trying to keep things for yourself and then giving, God asks us to *give* in order to *receive*. Jesus reminds us in the Gospel of Luke that it is more blessed to give than to receive. What does He mean by that? Why would it be more blessed to give than to receive, when it seems like such a joy to get things?

You've experienced little children on Christmas morning. Their eyes twinkle with the thrill and excitement of opening up packages and getting that one special present that they wanted. How can giving be more blessed than that? It's hard to explain, but in God's way of life for His children, giving is a thrill. Something happens in-side of us when we give that produces a joy that exceeds the joy of receiving. Think about it. When you see that child opening a present on Christmas morning, who has the most joy? When a friend is in need, and you stop by just to give a word of encouragement, who has the most joy?

How does that apply to us in terms of giving money when we are in so much trouble? Could God really expect us to give before we get back on our feet? This is where financial stability and financial wisdom are at their climax. The whole issue evolves around faith: trust that God is in control, and that He is so interested in our lives that He will take care of our needs and provide our financial requirements, not after we get in financial shape, but before.

Give the Firstfruits

God wants us to give of the *firstfruits* of our labors. In other words, He desires us to offer to Him the very first part of our income that we receive each month. In Proverbs 3:9-10, God says: "Honor the Lord with your wealth, with the firstfruits of all your crops; then your barns will be filled to overflowing, and your vats will brim over with new wine."

God sets up a reward for our giving. He promises to provide for our needs and to give to us so abundantly that we can't believe it. People talk about being cheerful givers and say that we should expect nothing in return. Yet God, in the Scriptures, says that, if we give, our barns will be full. In Malachi 3:10-11, He reiterates this again. If

*"Honor the Lord...with the firstfruits...
then your barns will be filled
to overflowing."*

Proverbs 3:9, 10

we give to God, then our barns and our vats will be full.

It is not natural for us to give. But God wants us to believe that as we give we can trust Him. There are so many pressured times when, financially, it doesn't seem like we should be giving because we just don't have enough money.

Give with Discipline

In 2 Corinthians, Paul tells us that God loves a cheerful giver but, more than that, God loves a giver. We often get confused on this point. We think, if we don't feel like giving, if we can't do it cheerfully, and if it is hard for us, then giving doesn't do us any good anyway, so we don't give. But God wants discipline in our lives, and there are many times when it *doesn't* feel good to give. We get an unusual bill or an illness in the family; our income decreases; our sales are not coming in like we thought they would; the car breaks down; it's Christmas time, and it is not very exciting to give. But God doesn't want us to stop giving at that point. He wants us to *trust Him*. That takes discipline and oftentimes that doesn't come cheerfully. Now, the more frequently we do it, in a disciplined way, the more cheerful we will become. Why? Because it is more blessed to give than to receive and our barns are going to be fuller than we could even imagine.

What does it mean to have our barns full? First, we must realize that some people have bigger barns than others. Thus, whatever size barn God has provided us (made up of needs +

resources + capacity to manage the resources) will be full. We will have a sufficient amount of resources to carry us through the winter. We will have freedom to rest at night and know that we have enough to carry us through. Our finances will be stabilized and other, non-financial, satisfactions may also be given to us. We will have a fulfilled life. It doesn't necessarily mean that we will be wealthy or that we will be poor. A farmer whose barns are full has a certain freedom to know that the next crop can be bad and he will still have financial stability. That is the kind of freedom God wants to give us. Freedom starts by giving. God wants to prove to us that He can out-give us.

Give as a Steward

As we mentioned previously, we are stewards of all that God has given us. That means that we are not controlling our own funds, but that we are managing God's funds. Whatever amount of resources He has given us, He wants us to manage properly.

What is the amount that we are supposed to be giving? Is it 10 percent? In the Old Testament, God did focus on a tithe, which is giving 10 percent. However, if we stick to a legalistic approach, we could add up all the different amounts that the Israelites were told to give and it could be as high as 22 percent.

Stretch Your Giving

The principle that God wants us to learn is stretching: giving of our firstfruits more than we are right now; trusting that God will take care of us financially, spiritually, emotionally, and psychologically; trusting that He will fill our barns and give us freedom. Again, we need to reiterate the point that if we give to God we will not necessarily be wealthy, but our needs will be taken care of. Our joys will be great. Our barns will be full and we will have freedom, freedom from the pressure of finances.

I use 10 percent as my stretch mark. I try to give at least 10 percent of my gross pay every month. I don't believe that there is any hard and fast rule that 10 percent is the magic number. Primarily, it is a matter of stretching to give more to God and trusting that He will come through with his promises. So, if you are giving only 1 percent, start giving 2 percent. If you are giving 2 percent, give 3 percent or 4 percent. Begin trusting the Lord. A tithe is a good goal. But once you get to that point, you will see that even more will be possible. I read where one individual set up a corporation and gave 50 percent of his income to the Lord. His company was blessed beyond measure.

To most of us, the issue is to establish giving as a priority. I can only tell you that every person I know who has followed this principle, who has started giving regularly to God and stretching more than they even thought they could give, was given financial freedom within a period of time. Why? Because God's promises are real.

When my wife, Linda, and I were first learning this principle, it was hard. Linda and I had been Christians for about eight to twelve months and we had gotten ourselves in real trouble. I had graduated from the University of Southern California with a master's degree in business economics, so I knew all about finances and managing money. Yet, the first thing I did was to get myself in trouble. I had received unrequested credit cards in the mail, which was common in 1972. Suddenly, I could buy cars, clothes, and other things, and eat out, all on MasterCharge. I even bought our first house on MasterCharge. That's quite a trick! Pretty soon I was up to my credit limit and could hardly pay my credit card minimum payments.

After I became a believer, I decided that I should start getting my financial ship in order. So I started giving as much as a dollar a week to God. He knew I was broke, He knew I was in trouble, and certainly He knew that I couldn't give Him more than that. I couldn't even afford to provide for my wife and daughter — to pay the house payment, utilities, food, and the other things — plus pay off the MasterCharge and all the other credit cards I had. I thought that I should wait until God blessed me financially before I started giving Him more than a dollar a week. I felt comfortable with that.

Then, on my way to work, I began listening to a Christian radio station and, every day for a week, somebody talked about giving and tithing: the importance of it, the joy of it, and the rewards of it, including feeling satisfied and being blessed by God. I thought that was really interesting, but that they probably were talking to people who had a lot more money and were in better financial shape than I was. I didn't think much more about it, other than just listening and acknowledging that it was there in the Scriptures.

The next Saturday night, at a friend's house, we started talking about their experience with giving and how they were giving 10 percent of their income to God and had been blessed with freedom and real stability. I thought to myself, "That's great for you guys, because you are older than we are and you have been making more money than we have." They had a couple of houses. I thought, "Yeah, you have extra income, so it's easy for you to give, but it certainly doesn't apply to me, at least not yet." The next night, Sunday, we went to church and our pastor, Dick Bush, gave a sermon on, you guessed it, tithing — the joys of it. He went through all the Scripture of God's actual commandment and His desire to have us give first.

Trust God Now and Give

On the way home, Linda and I decided that the whole issue was that of trust, that we really hadn't been trusting God. We were waiting for God to do something before believing that He would take care of us so that we could give back to Him. The scripture says clearly, if we give of our firstfruits, then He will fill our barns and our vats.

When we got home, Linda and I got down on our knees and prayed. We sensed that God wanted us to trust Him, to give Him the firstfruits of our income, to trust that He was really in control and that He is sovereign. This is the real issue.

God can manage our money *with* us, as opposed to us, by ourselves, trying to control and manipulate everything. Think about this a moment. Do you believe that God is in control of your life, which includes your finances, your satisfaction, and your business? Do you believe it? If so, it doesn't mean that you won't have financial hardship, but it does mean that you can have freedom.

What we prayed that night was that we would commit to giving 10 percent of our gross income. If we were going to be blessed, we wanted to be blessed on a gross basis and not on our net. We committed that we would do this, even though we knew our budget didn't have enough to take care of our bills. But we believed that it would not be us who would take care of our bills, but God!

We committed ourselves to that on Sunday night. The next Friday, I was called in by my boss, who said, ''Rich, you know you have been doing a pretty good job. We have never done this before in the history of our company. Even though we gave you your regular raise three months ago, I feel like I should give you another raise of 12 percent!'' We hadn't even written a check out for God, but only made the commitment in our hearts. God looks at the heart, not at the surface. He saw what we were committed to do and that we believed Him. He came through in His promise. We had enough money to give to God and still live on the rest.

I will share the rest of my story throughout the rest of the book. There wasn't an immediate production of wealth, because my wife and I suffered immensely for about eighteen months. But it all began with the principle of giving to God.

Give to Whom?

To whom or to what do we give? God doesn't physically come and take our money. So, what does giving to God mean? We have struggled over this issue through the years. We feel that our priorities are as follows: We give most of our tithe to the church. The church is God's primary form in New Testament times to spread the Gospel and to bring people into His kingdom. So, I believe that our first priority should be to our local church. Of course, that puts the responsibility on us to be satisfied that our local church is spending the money wisely, that it is active in evangelism, promotes fellowship, preaches the Word, and is not wasting its money or resources.

Next, we give to para-church organizations that are productive in furthering the Kingdom of the Gospel. The first ones are those we are involved in personally. I am very active in the Christian Business Men's Committee. This is a group that is committed to evangelizing, discipling and studying the Word with other men at regular meetings. I am very committed to this ministry. So, this group is one of my next priorities in giving. After that, there are other ministries that touch my life, such as radio ministries. Certain friends of ours are missionaries in various organizations such as Campus Crusade For Christ, SIM, and World Vision. I give to them because I know them. They write me and I know that they are committed to the ministry.

I think God can touch your hearts and give you a real sense of fullness as to which ministries you should support. They should include ones that are of interest to you, ones in which you can get active, and ones in which you see productivity. This means that it is your responsibility to find out how these ministries spend their money. There are a lot of so-called Christian ministries that do nothing more than promote their own organizations or provide wealth for the people in their ministries. They are not spending their money wisely.

I always ask ministries for a purpose statement, a statement of how they function, and then a financial report of the ministry. If they refuse to give these to me, I refuse to give. It usually means that they are hiding something. God does not want us to support things that are non-productive or that are not truly interested in furthering the Kingdom. We must be very careful to pray about this. Every year Linda and I review which ministries we are giving to and look at their priorities. Sometimes we take some off the list that we don't feel we should give to any more. As the Lord blesses me with more income, I have an opportunity to give more to those priorities that I have already selected and perhaps add other ones.

One thing to remember is that, if you do want tax deductions, you need to record your giving with checks. Also, you cannot give to a missionary directly, but must give to his organization and designate it for him on the envelope.

Besides tax deductible expenditures, there is another priority. This took a while for me to understand: to give as God presents the opportunity to me. By now, I was very disciplined in giving to the church and to the para-church organizations. I was giving my tithe and I felt good about it. But I had developed a bit of a rut and was giving regularly without thinking about those around me in need. So, I began praying that God would give me sensitivity to those around me who had a need that I could meet with my time or with my finances. Then I just relaxed and let God bring before me people and situations that needed money.

The principle, again, is giving first to God and to those that need it. As we do that, we will be blessed beyond measure. Our barns will be full, and we will begin the path toward financial freedom. Our satisfaction with life will begin to really increase. Other priorities are meaningless without taking care of this one first, because this says to God, "I believe you, I trust you and I know that you are going to take care of our needs. So I am going to give back the resources that you are allowing me to have."

Psychiatric Comment:

The *obsessive or perfectionistic* individual is known for the 3 P's. He is pecuniary (money-minded), parsimonious (excessively frugal), and pedantic (ruled by details). In other words, giving is not his strong point by nature. The one thing that seems to overcome his insecurity is money. Therefore, he is hesitant to let it go.

The *narcissistic* individual wants to be given to. He feels that he deserves more than he actually does. He feels "entitled."

The *paranoid* individual does not trust others. He feels they do not deserve what he might give them.

May we give more than the obsessive but with more planning than the hysteric. May we give rather than just receiving, as the narcissistic person does. May we give graciously and joyfully (2 Cor. 8).

CHAPTER SIX

Principle 3: Save Second

Our next priority, after giving to God first and demonstrating our trust in Him, is to act prudently in accordance with God's commandments regarding saving. We are actually to give to ourselves next.

Save at the Beginning

In our consumer-oriented society, saving is something we do at the end of the month or pay period, if we have anything left over. So most of us are not in a process of consistently putting money away for ourselves. The most common argument by evangelicals against saving is (as we saw in the last chapter) that God is going to take care of us, so we need not worry about saving. We can just go month to month with no reserve and trust that God will provide our needs as He promises.

This, however, is in contrast to God's Scripture concerning prudence. He says that all of us are going to face "drought times" sometime in our lives. And He says, very specifically, that His will for our lives is to save for those times.

None of us are exempt from potential financial problems. Even those who work for corporations can testify of being terminated and having no job for a period of time. One of my bosses worked for a major corporation. He was very successful with that firm for twenty years. But after having a personality clash with one of the leaders, he was asked to leave in a matter of minutes. So, none of us can find security in financial wealth or in our jobs. We must be prepared for the future and those drought times that are going to come.

God gave us commandments concerning saving. In Genesis 41:35, 36, He tells the story of Joseph, who was told by God directly that there would be a drought or a famine in Egypt. He was told specifically to save up for seven years and store away goods so that he would have enough food to last for all the people during this seven-year famine. As a result of this process, his father, Jacob, and his brothers were restored to him, because they, in fact, had not saved. They didn't think that a famine would come. Proverbs 21:20 says that there is stored food and oil in the house of the wise. And Jesus tells us, in the parable of the lampstand, that the foolish are the ones that spend or use everything and the wise are the ones that save it. He also tells us that the ant is the wisest animal, because he saves and stores up in the summer for the winter that is going to come.

God asks us to use our common sense in His commandments concerning saving. He wants us to store up resources so that, when financial difficulty comes upon us, we have the freedom to know that we can withstand it. This is particularly important for wives. If we did a survey of women, we would find that 80 percent of them rank security as one of their top values. When you have no resources in the bank, this produces real financial pressure on the wife. It nags at her and produces anxiety. She fears that something may happen in the future for which there will not be resources to pay for it. You may have to liquidate belongings, sell the house, or do other things to try to keep above water. Oftentimes we are faced with changing jobs. All of a sudden we need to make more income, so we will move, go to a different city, or change our family from a church in which we have been secure. It may have been God's will for you to have saved money, so that your family could have avoided that trauma and stayed exactly where you were, without having to move to a different place.

Proverbs 28 tells us that stability comes from honesty and sensibleness. God wants us to be sensible by saving in the abundant times for the difficult times ahead. Again, this taxes discipline. What I do is to put away another 10 percent of my income into a savings account at the beginning of the month. Then I try to learn to live on the rest of my income (80 percent). I build up liquidity and stability. Oftentimes, at the end of a month, I run out of money and need to dip back into my savings. But eight to ten times out of the year, I don't have to do that, so I am building up for the "winter" months.

Save with Liquidity

How should we approach saving? The first thing we should do is remain liquid, that is, have our money available to us so that we can get at it the very next day. We should either have a savings account, a money market fund, or certificates of deposit where we have four to six months of income saved up. If you save 10 percent of your income every month, it would take three to four years to save four to six months, worth of income. But while you are working and receiving abundant income is the time to do it. Most people say, "Well, I'll just go ahead and invest and try to get a lot more money faster." God wants us to be prudent and to develop liquidity first before we worry about investments. If the investment doesn't go as well as planned, we still have a cushion. All of us can attest that we have expenses come up that are not usual — car expenses, doctor bills, books, children's expenses, unexpected replacement of appliances (a washer, dryer or refrigerator). This is where we get into trouble. If we have no cushion, then we go out and use credit. Then we get behind in bills and get into further financial difficulty.

So, it is important to build your liquidity so that, if your income drops, or if unusual expenses come, you have an extra cushion and need not fear or have anxious thoughts about the future.

For those who are on commission, liquid savings are even more important, because your incomes vary from month to month. When you are having good times, you need to be particularly prudent in putting away money. I would recommend that salesmen work at putting away perhaps even more—10 to 15 or 20 percent—into a savings account, when you are having a good month. Then, when those low months come, you still will have money. Again, keep these priorities: (1) give to God first, and (2) save second, even if your income is lower than usual, because you can always come back and pull it out at the end of the month if you need it. It is important to discipline yourself to do it every month and get used to living on the other 80 percent. If you do this, you will be amazed at how much and how fast that money builds up.

Save with Investments

Once you develop liquidity of four to six months' worth of income, then it will be important to move into some kind of investment program, consistently putting away funds in things that can grow faster than the money market. I am *not* talking about a "get rich quick" scheme. God warns specifically in Proverbs to stay away from any "get rich quick" scheme because they won't work, and they lead mostly to evil and poverty. A recent example of that is an auto producer who was trying to get rich too fast with his company and got into financial difficulty. So he did desperate things to raise capital and it led to evil and poverty. Another fallacy that most of us fall into is borrowing money to get into investments. We put ourselves in double jeopardy then because, if the investment doesn't work out, we not only owe the money, but often we are liable for more money. So, invest only after you have a reasonable amount of money put away in liquid form and then move into a consistent, conservative, investment program that will allow you to build financial stability for your future.

Investments are perhaps the most difficult thing to make money in. Why? Because most of us are not skilled in researching, understanding, and deciding upon which investments will be successful. People who are trying to sell investments make promises and say things that aren't necessarily accurate. They usually make them sound more flowery than they really are.

Our firm currently has two or three investment groups and we look at many, many types of investments. We have partnerships whereby individuals can put an amount of money monthly into a mutual fund of real estate investments. This allows someone who doesn't have a lot of cash, but who has a little excess money to invest, to build equity for the future. I review approximately ten to fifteen investment opportunities a month for our firm. Of those ten to fifteen, only three or four are worth looking at. Of those three or four, maybe one is worth investing in.

Seek Expert Advice

A key for prudent investment is to seek wise counsel. God tells us to do this in Proverbs 12, Proverbs 20 and 1 Corinthians 5. He says victory will be won with the counsel of the wise. There is victory in many counselors. In an area such as this, it is essential that you have expert counsel guide you in a prudent investment program. To minimize your risk, consistently build investments that will make money. Most of us are very impatient regarding financial gain. But if we would look at our lifetime as having perhaps forty, forty-five, or fifty productive working years and we begin to invest early, by the time we are fifty or sixty years old we will be amazed at how much money we have put away.

Secondly, our house should be our primary investment. By building an equity in our house over a period of years we can sell it when our children leave us. Then we will have excess cash. Only two percent of all the people in the U.S.A. retire on a satisfactory income to enjoy life in the way they were accustomed to during their productive years. This is probably one of the saddest statistics in our culture today.

God gives us very specific instructions concerning this. If we just save and invest consistently and let our assets build on a progressive basis, over a period of time, our wealth will begin to accumulate. We won't be putting at risk those things that we worked so hard to gain.

What types of investments should we look at? Real estate is usually a very good one, although there are many markets where prices are decreasing. So, again you have to be careful. Stocks and bonds are sometimes good investments, but again you need wise counsel to help guide you through an economic analysis to see which ones make sense. Such things as oil wells and brand new companies are very, very risky. These should be invested in only with a small amount of risk capital that you are willing to lose. This should only be done when your investment portfolio is fairly stable. It is very important to diversify your investments into different avenues, so that you don't have all your eggs in one basket.

Another key aspect of investing is to let other people who are experts at it help you to manage it, so that it doesn't waste your time. This is another major source of frustration for families where the husband or wife is trying to manage outside investments and it is beyond their normal job. Instead of having quality time to spend with their family, they are spending excess time trying to manage investments that they feel they need to control. God would rather have us do no investing and spend quality time with our wives and children than spend our time trying to get rich or richer. So, don't be afraid to let other people do the work, those who are skilled at it and spend their lives at it. It will cost you some money, but is worth it.

Be sure you check out those people, however. And make sure their reputations are strong, that they have performed in the past, that they know what they are doing, that they follow Christian principles, and that they are investing in things that are not going to be detrimental to the glory of the Lord.

The parable of the talents is a very strong summary of this area of saving and investing. God rewarded those according to the amount of resources he gave each, and they went out and multiplied their resources. The one who hid it and just stuck it away was penalized. God expects us to be prudent, to be investing, and to save for the winter that is about to come.

Psychiatric Comment:
Saving comes easily for the obsessive-compulsive individual. It is difficult for the hysterical individual. Being pecuniary (money-minded) is a characteristic of the obsessive. A lack

of planning is a characteristic of the hysteric. The obsessive never wants to let go of his savings. He saves for the future — the future that never comes. The hysteric lives only for today, there is no tomorrow. Both extremes are dangerous. This is why the wise individual seeks expert advice, objective counsel, regarding his savings.

CHAPTER SEVEN

Principle 4:
Provide Family Needs

After we have demonstrated our faithfulness by giving to God first and then giving to ourselves (by saving) second, the next priority is to take care of our basic family needs. God is very specific on this point in 1 Timothy 5:8 where He tells us that those who don't take care of their own families are worse than unbelievers. In the Old Testament, the family unit was a prime social entity. Taking care of the family's basic needs was of utmost importance. This encompassed everyone from grandparents to children. In Luke 11, God tells us that even evil people take care of their children. God tells how much greater He is than this, and that He wants to take care of us. Therefore, using this as an example, we need to have the same desire and sensitivity to meeting the needs of our own family.

One area that families don't spend much time discussing is the true meaning of "basic needs." What is really important to us? We can break this down to include housing, food, clothing, automobile, and transportation. Since we all need these things, the key is to fit these needs within the amount of resources that God has given us. Thus, our total needs, if we listed them and could quantify them, should be no more than 40 to 50 percent of our income. A breakdown might be as follows: If you take your income and divide it in half, then that is the amount of money you should have available as a maximum for your basic needs. Then work out the different items within that to see the level at which you can spend to meet your family needs.

Taking care of your family means having freedom and security, and being at ease. God says in Proverbs 1 that if you want to have security, ease, and safety, then seek wisdom and be prudent. He also tells us in James that we are not to presume on the future. We are in a society that says we will make more money tomorrow than we did yesterday and inflation will make our payments of less value if we stretch ourselves and buy on credit today. This is a fallacy that built up during a very short period of high inflation in the U.S. economy. However, if you travel through Europe, you will see that the values of houses stay pretty much the same. Many areas in the U.S., even now, are seeing houses depreciate. This is particularly true in California, where many people bought houses on speculation only to get caught with payments that they couldn't meet, particularly on loans with balloon payments.

The Need for Housing

Let's take the first primary need: housing. Housing should cost us no more than 25 to 30 percent of our total income or about half the amount we have allocated for our family needs. This should include utilities, taxes, repairs, any maintenance such as lawn care or pool care, insurance, and the phone bill. The key is to choose housing that will fit our particular budget. This may mean that some of us need to move to different living quarters. We find ourselves already strapped with high payments that really stretch us. Many of us are looking to upgrade and have the desire for a bigger and better house. We may need to wait for this until we have the income to support it.

Another area to consider is the financing arrangements. Often we have purchased houses with second mortgages and balloon payments thinking that we will sell them before we need to pay the balloon. Time comes around for the balloon to be paid and we haven't sold the house. All of a sudden we are faced with foreclosure. I would urge you not to obtain housing that has second mortgages. If you can't afford the primary mortgage on a monthly basis, then I don't believe it is God's will for you to have that house. God said it is better to have little with peace than to have great things and anxiety.

This is not to say that, if God is blessing you financially, a larger house is against His will. He may want to put you in a more expensive neighborhood, because He is interested in expanding His Kingdom to all people, which includes the wealthy. But He is more interested in our well-being and He wants us to be at peace so that we will have the freedom to minister for Him. High interest rates will continue and will probably never drop below 11 or 12 percent again. So, please consider those amounts when you are looking for financing.

Another consideration is repairs on housing. If you decide that you can afford only an older, lower-priced house, consider that there may be a lot of things wrong with it (such as wiring, broken appliances, heaters, etc.). These repairs cost extra money. So, be careful when you buy an older house. You may want to consider purchasing a new house where special financing opportunities are available, one where the builder is paying the financing points, which enables you to get a low down payment. This would be good as long as monthly payments are within the budget you have specified.

If you are in deep financial straits because of a house, seriously come before God and ask Him if He would like you to sell it and move to different quarters. All of us can find satisfactory housing that will meet our needs. Again, you may want to consider what is important to your family. If you like the outdoors, if you like large yards, then you might want to move to the country. If you enjoy the city and its activities, you might want to move closer in.

A guideline that Linda and I always have utilized is to find our church first. We locate where we find a church that is satisfactory to our family, one where we are being fed on a continual basis with the Word and with good fellowship, and our children have good youth groups. We want to have our children live in the same neighborhood with the school children who go to church with them, so that they will have a strong Christian peer group. We would rather have a smaller house near our church than to get a bigger one far away. I know of one case where an individual bought a bigger house which was far away from his friends and church. After he moved, his family began to fall apart, because relationships with friends and church just weren't the same. God is more interested in our relationships than in our material belongings. Getting better and bigger things is *not* more satisfying. *Things* do *not* make happiness.

The Need for Food

The next area to look at is the food budget. We all fall into different patterns here. The key would be to really scrutinize where you spend your money. See if you are wasting your money on junk food and other items that really are not good for you. We can all probably reduce our eating, anyway. Be prudent and go to the stores where you can get the best buys consistently. Don't shop when you are hungry, so that you won't buy too much. Plan out meals ahead of time, so that your expenditures make sense. Probably, you should include lunch money for the kids and, if you go out to eat regularly during the week, then you should include that in the food budget.

The Need to Pay Taxes

The next item would be taxes. This is particularly important for those on commission who receive gross income and do not pay withholding taxes. I have many friends on sales commissions who, on April 15, always have difficulty, because they haven't saved the money to pay their income taxes. This is a basic need because it is required by law. We need to put aside money for state taxes, federal taxes, and any personal property taxes. Don't let this become a burden to you later.

The Need for Transportation

Another area is transportation. Most of us are stuck with the automobile as a means of transportation. This can become a very large expenditure. Automobiles are poor investments. We have to look at them as an expense, because they depreciate significantly. We need to look at our automobile strictly as a necessity for transporting us from place to place. We don't need the best, biggest, or fanciest, but one that will meet our budget.

This is a good place to digress to depreciating items. Under *no* circumstances use debt or loans to purchase depreciating items. Why? Because if we had to sell them, we would not be able to pay back the amount that we owe on them. This becomes true debt, and we will see in the next chapter why God doesn't want us to become involved in that. Since an automobile is a depreciating item, the rule I go by is not to borrow more than one-half the value of the automobile, so that my payments will always be ahead of the value of the car. If I had to sell it or trade it in, I could pay it off and not have an extra burden.

Included in the transportation budget are the cost of gasoline, insurance and repairs. Repairs is a key area to look at. See how much you have been spending in repairing an old automobile. It may be better to go ahead and purchase a new car and keep away from those repair bills. A good rule of thumb is to trade in your automobile after two-and-a-half to three years when you have the opportunity to maximize your trade-in value. Usually that is the time when repair bills start to increase.

This is a good case for saving and trusting God. If automobiles are one of your higher priorities, then it is important to start putting the money away now and trusting God to keep the old klunker going until you have enough money to meet this guideline. If you do have an opportunity to buy a more expensive car, it may be more beneficial, because they frequently depreciate less. Nonetheless, when you go to purchase an automobile, really research and spend the time to see that you are getting the best buy. Don't go on emotion as to what looks best to you. Look at the history, look at performance ratings. Review the kind of warranties provided. Check to see that you are getting the most for your money.

The Need for Furniture

The next area is furniture. Obviously, within your house you will need furniture. Again, the key is to provide the basic family needs, but not to use loans to purchase furniture. You can sell furniture for only a fraction of its value. So, be content with what you have. If you would like to upgrade or fill a room, this is where savings again becomes important. You ask God for it, save for it so that you can get the best buy, and get it free and clear when you do purchase it.

When my wife and I were young, and I was working for a large corporation, we moved into a house that had a living room and a family room. We had enough furniture for the family room but not enough for the living room. We left the living room empty until the time that we were able to save enough money to pay cash for the items that we wanted.

We continually work at saving for furniture and upgrade with nice things that will last a long time. We are building slowly, item by item, and add only when we have the money to pay for it.

The Need for Clothing

Next is clothing. All of us need clothes. Our appearance is important. I believe that God wants us to present our best self and demonstrate that we are qualified and presentable as co-workers who are believers. Being a Christian does not mean that we have to wear rags. At the same time, we don't have to go overboard and have the most expensive wardrobe. We just need one that will compliment us and make us presentable.

This is particularly true for school children who have much peer pressure with their clothes. Meeting a family need here means not setting them up for ridicule. You may say, "Well, peer pressure puts emphasis on designer clothes and all those things that are too expensive. We just can't afford it."

In our family we set aside a certain amount of money for clothes. We then give that amount of money to our children and tell them they are free to purchase whatever clothing they would like to have for the school year. When they run out of money, they can't buy any more clothes. They become very prudent quickly as to where they are going to spend their money. It is exciting to watch them become skilled buyers, when they know they are going to run out of resources. If they feel that designer clothes are important to them, they get a few, but that is their limit. This needs to be geared, of course, to the ages of your children.

Another principle that we use, when we are building a wardrobe, is to do it by paying cash. We don't use loans, because you can't sell clothes at all. We add things to our wardrobe periodically, instead of going overboard in trying to replace clothes or meet fads. We just add occasionally with conservative clothes that will fit any particular style. We buy fewer and nicer clothes so that they will last longer. By no means use loans or credit cards to buy clothes. If we can't afford it, then God doesn't want us to have it right now.

The Need for Education

The next area to look at is education. Education is a prime value in our society. God wants our children to be educated and to go into fields that will enable them to witness to the world. We need to provide financing for our children's education. Those of you who have sons or daughters in college know what I am talking about. All of a sudden it is on us and we have to borrow money to pay for their tuition, room and board. It would be more prudent to plan for their future by saving up each month while they are young, so that you won't have that burden when they need to go to school. Some of us may have special education for our children that is important and this needs to be budgeted in this amount. Many of us have children that are involved in extra-curricular activities, such as gymnastics, skating, tennis, or music—things that are important to the children and would require lessons. We need to budget that, as well.

The Need for Insurance

A final note under basic needs is insurance — health insurance, life insurance, and disability insurance. What if the bread winner of the family should die (and none of us knows when that will happen)? I was made more aware of this just recently when I went into the hospital with severe stomach pain. I was diagnosed as having stomach poisoning. After going home, I had the same pain a week later. I went back to the hospital and they decided to keep me there for tests. That night the doctor walked in and said that my gall bladder was diseased and that, if he didn't operate immediately, I would have a chance of dying within twenty-four hours. The fact that the doctor happened to be there that night to look at me made the difference of my continuing to live here on earth or going to be with the Lord. I thought quite a bit about how life is "but a vapor" and there is no guarantee that we will be here tomorrow. The need for the family is to have the bread winner provide for the possibility of not being here tomorrow. Some rules of thumb are:

(1) Provide disability insurance so that 60 percent of your income can be covered.

(2) Provide enough health insurance, with no more than a two- to five-hundred-dollar deductible, so that a major disaster won't wipe you out financially. For example, the gall bladder operation that I just had cost seven thousand dollars. If I had not had insurance to pay for it, I would have experienced quite a financial loss.

(3) Multiply your yearly income times ten and purchase that much life insurance. This is approximately the amount of income you should provide for your spouse so that the money could be invested in safe instruments such as a money market fund to continue to provide income annually after you are gone.

The Need for a Will

Another important need is to have a will corresponding with this insurance to designate how the funds are to be spent and invested. This is particularly critical for women when their husbands die. Women are bombarded immediately by people who try to take advantage of them with so-called "investments." Something like 75 percent of life insurance proceeds are wasted within the first two to three years because there has been no provision as to how best to spend it.

I recommend that you set up a trust, whereby the money is not given to your spouse in a lump sum, but where they receive the income from it yearly. Special provisions should be made for college educations, special needs, etc., but most of the money should be preserved so that the spouse can work through the grieving process properly and not be burdened financially. Also, in this way, the money will not be quickly spent. I also suggest that your will designate a financial advisor to help the wife spend and invest the money prudently. This relieves a great deal of pressure in planning what the needs are, what the desires were of the deceased, and how best to plan for the family's future.

If you don't develop a will, the government decides how your money is to be spent. This takes time, also. I recommend that you have this as a primary item, even for smaller amounts of money, particularly to make sure that you minimize your estate taxes.

The key to family needs is to prioritize what things are important to you. Where, geographically, is it going to be comfortable for you to live? How far is that from your church and friends? (Remember that relationships are more important than having big spaces.) What are the most important needs for your children and your spouse? Is your wife interested in going back to school and getting her education now that the kids are grown? If this is an important need for her at this time, put that in the budget. What things are important to your family? In terms of your needs, do you want to be able to take special lessons or to get that new automobile or to build your wardrobe? What is most important for you? Put this on top of your prayer list. Then begin to save money for that. In Chapter 10, we will focus on the process of how to spend wisely.

Psychiatric Comment:

The *obsessive* provides well financially for his family but not emotionally. He gives of his means but not of his emotions. He gives of his money but not of his time. His workaholism provides for financial needs, but this can prove fatal to the family.

The *hysteric,* too, may have more trouble providing for emotional family needs than financial ones, though the financial too can be a problem because of lack of planning. (The hysteric, in search of deep emotional closeness, may be easy prey for affairs, never to learn that surface emotions don't fill deep emotional needs.)

Both of these personalities, starting from their own weaknesses, need to seek a balance in providing for both the financial and emotional needs of their families.

CHAPTER EIGHT

Principle 5: Pay Off Debt

I'm sure that most of you have experienced being over-involved with too much debt. This is a difficult area to understand in Scripture, because God tells us not to be a borrower, while telling us in other places that it is okay to lend money. Deuteronomy 23:19 was a real enigma to me. How could God say that we can go ahead and lend money but, in Romans 13:8, we are told not to borrow? He says don't be in debt to anyone. Finally, through much prayer and thought, I believe God gave me the answer.

The Definition of Debt

Debt is not equal to loans. Debt is defined as when the value of what you own, your asset, is less than the amount you owe on that asset. For example, if you buy a thousand dollar couch, and you borrow a thousand dollars to purchase it, the day that you buy it the value of the couch is one thousand dollars and what you owe on it is one thousand dollars. Theoretically, you have no debt. On the second day that you own that couch, it is now worth only eight hundred dollars and you still owe a thousand dollars, so you are in debt by two hundred dollars.

This is what God is saying when He tells us that we are to have no debt whatsoever–none. We are not to owe more on an asset than the current value for which we could sell that asset. Why does God tell us this? Because He loves us and wants us to have financial freedom.

Debt Produces Slavery

The most important reason against debt is given in Proverbs 22:7, where the borrower (the person in debt) is said to be a slave to the lender. The word "slave" means that you have constant pressure to do what the master wants. You are always worried and constantly concerned about what might happen. I am sure that many of you can testify that, when you go to bed at night, you worry about paying back all those loans. What will happen if your income decreases, or if you get fired, or if your bills increase. You are always living on the brink of disaster.

It produces an anxiety that creates pressure for the entire family. If we are in constant anxiety over finances, we don't have the chance to work through some of our other normal anxieties and fears. We all need to develop unity in our family. So, the most important reason against debt, as defined, is that it produces undue pressure and undue anxiety through bondage that God doesn't want us to experience.

James 4:1 tells us that we are not to say that we will go and do this or that tomorrow, but rather say, "if the Lord wills." His will may be for us to be available for a different cause or ministry, but because of our financial situation, we are forced to ignore His will. This correlates directly with 1 Timothy 5:8 that says, if we don't take care of our families, we are worse than unbelievers. For many families, the pressure is almost insurmountable.

Buying on Credit Limits God

Also, presuming that we can just buy whatever we want on credit limits God. It never gives Him an opportunity to provide for us. Second Corinthians 9:11 says specifically that God wants to bless us and demonstrate His faithfulness to us. If we are constantly using credit cards and loans to buy things, and not bringing them before the Lord first, we don't give Him a chance to demonstrate that He really loves us and can and will take care of us. In Luke 11 it says that God is far better than evil fathers who give their children things to make them happy. God wants to demonstrate His love and faithfulness.

We find this to be particularly important in teaching our children that God is interested in our lives. We have a scrapbook of things that are on our priority prayer list. The many, many miracles that our children have seen from this have been phenomenal. It really demonstrates to them that God is in control and wants to bless us.

We had a station wagon, a Ford Pinto, that had been rapidly deteriorating. We put a new car in our scrapbook and began praying for one. I knew that I wouldn't buy one for more than half the value, so we began saving for it. Every week on our prayer list we asked God to provide us a car. We prayed for this for a year, but still decided that we were not going to go out and violate the principles that we had learned. After a year, I found myself doing some consulting work for a

developer in California who had an extra Mercedes Benz. He came to me one day wanting to thank me for all the work I had done for him. He said, "I have this extra car. Would you please take it?" God answered our prayer and demonstrated to our family that God is interested and provides beyond measure.

Psychiatric Comment:

The *obsessive* would not tend to have problems with debt unless it was in one of his areas of extremes. The obsessive is pulled between extremes and opposite traits. He is conscientious in some areas and negligent in others. He is orderly in some areas and untidy in others. He is usually obedient but occasionally defies. He is probably debt free but possibly debt enslaved.

The *hysteric* may have trouble paying off debt. Whereas the obsessive's conscience is so rigid that he makes himself miserable, the hysteric may need to strengthen his conscience and sense of responsibility.

One personality type that may have trouble on both ends of the spectrum is known as the *cyclothymic*. He alternates between being high and being low. When high, he feels so good his judgment is impaired. He may buy too much, pay off too little. When low, he is overly strict on himself and worries incessantly over any debt.

CHAPTER NINE

Principle 6:
Spend Wisely

We are all faced with the necessity of buying things for everyday living for our family, all the way from major items, like houses and cars, to minor items, like socks and underwear for our children. Even after we have established the correct priorities, as we discussed previously, how to spend is where most of us get into trouble. No one has ever given us a course on how to buy things or on the spending process of money. So we follow patterns that we have been manipulated into, mostly by television.

Advertising Affects Spending

The average family today watches seven hours of television a day. If you are at that level, then you are receiving well over two hundred buying messages per day. This is in addition to those that you receive over the radio on the way to work and back, or out driving errands. There are also newspapers, billboards, and magazine ads. All of these media that we review are built economically on advertising, so that at least half of what we look at, review, or read is filled with messages to purchase things.

Madison Avenue advertisers are skilled at motivating us to buy things. Why do you think car advertisements have such beautiful, sensual women standing next to the cars? It arouses our emotions. When our emotions are stimulated, we are more likely to buy. Why do department stores, at the point of check out, display small items? These are called impulse items. They know that, as you walk by, you will have a tendency to feel an impulse to pick them up and add them to the things that you are purchasing. Do you ever wonder why, at night, you have a tendency to want to go to a fast-food place or order a pizza? The next time you watch TV after 8:00 P.M., watch all the food ads. Then you will begin to understand why your juices start salivating and you want certain foods! Our whole society is built upon motivating people to purchase things.

Even though we have a deep faith in the Lord and are constantly seeking to avoid materialism, we cannot help but be exposed to these messages and react to them just as any normal person. Just because we are Christians does not mean we are exempt from the natural stimulation that the experts are so good at triggering. Thus, with this constancy of buying messages all around us, every day of our lives, how can we possibly spend wisely? It requires discipline on our part to use consistently a spending process whereby we avoid spending unwisely.

Spending for Need or for Significance?

What is the difference in spending wisely and unwisely? Unwise spending occurs whenever we begin to yield to the lust of the flesh and the lust of the eyes, using *things* to bring us significance. Sometimes we put ourselves under

financial bondage for the sake of having *things* that won't really give us more than a moment's feeling of significance.

Wise spending occurs when we purchase only things that we *need*. Then we buy things that we *want* only when we have the financial resources to do so without placing ourselves under bondage. This means we should never borrow money to purchase anything that is depreciating in value (like cars) or to buy experiences (like trips or concerts). We should pay for these things only with our savings. (As stated earlier, it would be okay to borrow half of the purchase price of a car, since you could always sell it in an emergency for more than what you owed on it.

Principles of Wise Spending

The key to spending wisely is to utilize the following principles:

(1) *Ask the Lord first.* In today's society, something we *know* we should do but rarely work at is trusting *God* to provide us with *things*. We have a hard time seeing the correlation of *God* providing us things, when we know that we need to *buy* things with our *own* money. So we think, "How can God provide this for us? He is certainly not going to just hand it to us on a silver platter!" There is a very delicate balance between asking God for His will in a matter versus wanting God to be our *genie* and expecting Him to wave a magic wand to give us everything we want, especially if our parents spoiled us when we were growing up.

Matthew 7:7 clearly instructs us, "Ask and it will be given to you; seek and you shall find; knock and the door will be opened to you." Jesus illustrates this with a story of a father who gives good things to his children. James tells us that every good thing is from God. God gave us a beautiful world and many beautiful things for us to enjoy. God wants us to enjoy things in the proper perspective. "Ask and it will be given to you," follows a statement by Jesus made earlier in the Sermon on the Mount. "You cannot serve both God and money" at the same time (Matt. 6:24). These verses don't mean that God will give us everything that we want. Instead, they teach us that we should share our desires with God and depend upon Him to provide those things that *He* decides would be the best for us in the long run. Even the Apostle Paul had some of his prayer requests turned down.

Once we have the proper perspective in seeking God first; and not greed, power, and money; then we can ask God for things freely. And, being a good Father, He will give us the things that will bring us great satisfaction and benefit, just as we do for our own children.

Why does God want to bless us? Most of all, He wants to demonstrate to us that He is in control and that all good things do come from Him. He is interested in showing us that He is a great Father and wants to provide things that we need. As we develop a faith, trust, and thankfulness in our heart for the things that we have, God will trust us with even more and want to please us even more.

Think back to a relationship with a child. If children are ungrateful and don't seem to care about what they have and get, then we don't have a desire to give them more. But as they truly appreciate and take care of things, and come and ask us first for them, we have a strong desire to meet those needs and wants.

God is greater than we, as parents, and has the same desires. So, before you go and spend money, even if you have the cash to pay for it, ask the Lord first. Put it on your prayer list. Be patient. Let God demonstrate that He will provide all of your needs.

(2) *Develop sales resistance.* With all of the messages to buy things, and all of the opportunities to go shopping, particularly at shopping malls that we enjoy walking through, we need to develop a *resistance* to buying things. We must be able to check ourselves when we have an impulse to buy. When Linda and I have an impulse to buy something, we usually go home, think about it, and pray about it. The next day, if we still feel strongly about it, then we add it to our prayer list and ask God for it. Usually the impulse passes and we realize there is no need for it. This takes great discipline and much practice.

Another way to develop sales resistance is to avoid frequent visits to shopping malls and stores, since it is very difficult to counteract those natural stimulations that the advertisers try to create in us. Sometimes you may find it fun to visit a mall, particularly on a rainy day, but don't develop a habit of regularly going to a mall and walking through the stores. This can have a very interesting psychological effect. You see all that you would like to have (naturally, we all would like to have more) and the displays in the stores are designed to show us all those beautiful things that we "must have," so we wind up comparing what we have with what we would like to have and this develops into an actual depressant. You may have found yourself coming home from a mall worn out, tired, and a little depressed. It is probably because you realize that you may never have all of those things. Other times, we give in and use credit cards to buy those great things that will bring us supposed satisfaction, then we find that they never do.

Another way we develop sales resistance is to go shopping only for a specific need or want, so that we focus only on that one thing that we have already decided to buy. It helps if we have already decided how much money we are going to spend when we go to buy it. So, we calculate how much cash we have on hand to spend for that item. Then we go shop for it at that price or below. We have to be careful here, if we see the item we want at a little higher price than we are allowing ourselves to spend, to stay within our limit. I believe this is where we can trust in God's providence. We have prayerfully and thought-fully considered how much we are going to spend. We are asking God to provide that for us and we are not willing to go over that price.

When we found a piano we wanted to buy for our daughter, the price that the person was asking was slightly above what we were willing to pay. I told them the limit on the amount I was willing to pay. The salesman said he could not go that low. "Okay," I said, "that's fine." In my mind, I had already prayerfully thought through that limit and believed that God didn't want me to go over it. Then the seller came out the door and said, "Well, okay, I think I'll let you have the piano for that price." I had felt quite sure that God wanted us to buy that piano, but I was perfectly willing to walk away from it if the price wasn't right.

That is another principle I follow in negotiating certain things, such as houses and cars and major purchases, where you can bargain with the seller. In every negotiation, I am willing to go away from it and feel that I don't need to have it. If you go into a negotiation with that as a premise and establish the price that you are willing to pay, then you can walk away from the negotiation not feeling you have made a mistake or that it is the last deal in the world that you are ever going to have.

There is some inherent emotion in all of us that says, If we don't get this bargain now, we will never have another chance at one. This is particularly true with houses. I just counseled a doctor who was considering moving into a bigger house, had already made an escrow payment on it, and was told that the price of this house was $30,000 under the market. He felt that this was the only good deal in North Dallas that he would ever get a chance for. So, he was willing to sacrifice his financial freedom and become over-extended in order to purchase the house, because it was such a great deal. As we sat and talked through the process, he realized that he was not willing to trade his financial freedom for this deal.

One good way to set the limit, when we are buying such things as clothes, is to save up the money for the items or things that we are trying to buy. Then, take that much in cash with us (as opposed to checks) and, when we run out of cash, we are through buying. We do this for trips, Christmas, special occasions, and furniture. We establish an amount of money which we then save up for, then we go out and spend up to that limit. We wind up spending more wisely and avoid getting ourselves into financial bondage.

(3) *Get the best buy.* You need to get the best buy through comparison shopping. The very first thing you see is often the one that arouses your emotions. You often can do better with price and value by "shopping around." We take a little notebook when we are buying things valued at twenty dollars or more. Particularly with the convenience of shopping malls, we can go from store to store and compare prices. Even in the same mall, we often can find savings of 40 to 50 percent on the same item. We look around for that item that we are trying to purchase and determine which one has the best value and price. Then we go back and purchase it. It is really a lot of fun to go comparison shopping as a family. We get everyone involved. This is especially important when you are shopping for major items such as houses, cars, and vacations.

Another key factor to consider when purchasing things is that the lowest price is not necessarily the best. You need to look at how fast it will fall apart, the quality of it, and how long it will last. When purchasing clothes, you may find that the lowest priced clothing will, in fact, cost you more in the long run because it falls apart and needs to be replaced sooner. Use *Consumer Report* magazines to determine quality, serviceability, and reputation. This will be true of appliances and things that require fixing, so that you don't spend a great deal on repairs. You should compare warranty periods and reputation.

When purchasing services such as house repairs, roof repair, pool service, and lawn care, it is important to compare prices, get different bids, and do reference checking. Of course, if you ask someone to provide references, they are going to provide you with their very best references, if not relatives. So I say that I would like to talk to the last three customers done in the last month or two. If they give me those names and numbers, then I call them. If they are not willing to do that and say, "Well, I only had one this last month but I had some several months ago," it probably indicates that they have customers that aren't very satisfied or, in fact, that they haven't done much work.

(4) *Pay promptly.* If you do use credit cards and have learned to exercise discipline, pay for the entire credit card bill at the end of each month. If you use gas credit cards, pay the entire amount at the end of the month. Do not pay the minimum and develop a balance that creeps up, and up, and up, until finally you are in financial trouble. Keep your obligations on time every

month: house payment, car payment, utilities, telephone, etc. Do not get behind; make prompt payments. Then the cash that is left beyond those payments you can use to spend on the things that you need and want.

Proverbs 3:38 says that "A wise man pays promptly." So get in the habit of purchasing items with cash or through check so you will not have a tendency to get behind. You will realize that you have certain limits and that God is in control of your spending. If you don't have the cash available, then assume that God does not want you to purchase that item at this time. Perhaps the partial amount you had available for it should be saved to pay for more important things that will come up in the near future.

Communication with your spouse is also very important. List those things that are high priorities for you and take your time. My wife and I are remodeling our house. We sat down and listed all of the items that we would like to have over a period of time. We will pay cash for these and buy them in priority, which may take a year or two. We realize that there is no thrill in having these all at once and getting ourselves in financial bondage. Material satisfaction is a fleeting satisfaction. So, as we put it in perspective, we can enjoy the process of spending, leaving God in control, and avoiding financial bondage. By doing so, we have the great satisfaction and genuine self-respect that comes from *financial freedom*, rather than the guilt, fear and anxiety that comes from *financial bondage*.

Psychiatric Comment:

Spending wisely is a characteristic of a balanced personality. Spending wisely takes overcoming our *obsessive* traits that would cause us to hoard money and not spend at all. Spending wisely takes overcoming *hysterical* traits that would cause us to spend foolishly. Spending wisely takes overcoming *narcissistic* traits that would cause us to spend selfishly. Spending wisely takes overcoming *paranoid* traits that would cause us to spend grudgingly. Indeed, spending wisely takes a balanced personality.

CHAPTER TEN

Principle 7: Have Fun Money

You have gotten to this point and you probably think, "Boy, God must not want us to have any fun, because this is going to be hard. We're not going to have any money for just enjoyment. We're going to get bored and our life is going to be a real pain."

But I don't believe that God wants us to be sorrowful. He wants us to have an abundant life. John 10:10 says, "I have come that they may have life, and have it to the full." In Deuteronomy 6, God promised the nation of Israel that they would have their beautiful land, and much fruit and houses and prosperity, and enjoyment. So, God wants His people to have resources for enjoyment and to use these freely.

The Freedom to Enjoy

The freedom to enjoy life is the whole principle of following this prescribed money diet. By following it, you can become disciplined enough to have the financial freedom to enjoy the things God has provided for you.

I am sure we all can relate to times when we have gone out with the family to an amusement park and have had a hard time enjoying being with them, because of the bondage and pressure of finances. We have had money worries on our mind so we haven't been truly free to have fun with them. God wants us to be in a position to set aside fun money — monies that don't go to anything particular, that aren't building anything, or going toward investing, or even buying things, but that is just fun money to have experiences with.

The key principle, though, is that you *pay cash*. God wants us to have experiences, but He doesn't want us to get in bondage. So, under no circumstances are we to use credit cards or loans to purchase experiences that provide some fun for us.

Our family sets aside at least one day on the weekend or one night to go to different entertainment opportunities. We see such things as plays, an orchestra, or an entertainer, particularly if a Christian entertainer is in town.

Many of these things, by the way, are offered free. When we lived in Chicago, there would be a free concert at the Grant Park band shell on Lakeshore Drive several nights a week during the summer. We would take a blanket, spend the evening, and have a good time together for free.

We pick different restaurants, from low-cost, fast-food restaurants to expensive ones, to go out and eat together. We go to sporting events to see the Dallas Cowboys, Texas Rangers, Dallas Mavericks, or SMU Mustangs. Each year, we go to the Southwest Conference Basketball Tournament and Tennis Cup Tournament. We plan these a couple of months ahead. We also like to go to amusement parks. In the Dallas area, there are Six Flags and White Water, which has water slides and swimming. Because we enjoy going to

CITY ZOO

White Water so much, we purchase season passes, because they are cheaper in the long run. We save up for these and buy them in the spring.

There are other such places around the country. Many communities have beaches, lakes, and oceans where you can have fun times with your family. Certainly every community has a park. State parks and national parks also are meant for us to enjoy and these are very inexpensive.

We plan out our weekends a couple of weeks ahead and then set aside an amount of money in cash to go out and enjoy the day together. We use such times to solidify our family unit. Too often, in today's culture, the family is fractured and everyone goes in different directions. Individualism is promoted over the concept of the family unit and community. With our fun money, we consciously spend time together on outings, talking to one another, enjoying one another, and just being together as a family.

Date Your Mate

Another enjoyable experience to consider is to take your spouse on a date. This can go both ways, where the wife calls up her husband at work and says, "I'm going to take you out tonight, or she plans a special time that is a surprise. The husband can call his wife at work or at home and say, "I've arranged everything and we are going to go out tonight." Make it a really special event. This should happen at least once or twice a month. Time alone as a couple is important. This is why so many couples, even Christian couples, as they get older, wind up getting divorced. Frequently they have never spent quality time together and haven't developed the enjoyment of being together. As their children grow, all of a sudden there is an empty nest, and it is lonely. It's hard to get back in step with one another. So use your fun money to encourage the communication process between you and your spouse.

Vacation as a Family

Another key area is to consider a family vacation every year. Vacations should be spent as a unit with the children and both spouses. It is really surprising to see so many couples go on separate vacations. The man may go with the boys and the woman with the girls to different places. This would be fine on occasion, but not if it excludes family vacations with everyone together. Personally, we plan the time that we have off from our work. Usually, we have some in the summer and a little bit in the winter. We schedule places that our family would like to go. We get brochures and write to the chamber of commerce in that area or get information from a travel agency. Next, we try to determine how much cash we have available and how much we need to save up for our vacation. Then we plan ahead. We pick places that are going to be stimulating to us.

Some people use their vacations to visit relatives. You need to be careful with that, however. If you feel anxious around your relatives, then you defeat the purpose of your vacation by visiting them. Each family unit, of course, must decide that for themselves.

Vacations should be a relaxing time and should be at least one to two weeks, ideally two weeks. Wind down, get away from work, and spend quality time together, enjoying one another and relaxing. A lot of people don't take vacations because they "can't afford it." This should be a high priority for all of us. We need our rest, we need our times to get away to keep our perspective on life and on what life is all about.

Along with vacations would be weekend excursions, particularly when you have long weekends available. It could even be to a local hotel downtown to explore and look at museums, walk down the streets, and enjoy the people and parks. We plan at least one weekend excursion a quarter and oftentimes will rent a friend's cabin. We take our own food and spend the weekend in the woods relaxing.

As a matter of fact, that is what I am doing right now as I write this book. We are up in the woods for a weekend during spring break. It has been a beautiful time together. We have enjoyed a thunderstorm, we have enjoyed going fishing, boating, and playing volleyball. It has been a really relaxing time for our family just to get away.

We also enjoy going on "one-night stands" in downtown Dallas. We stay at a hotel and get the special weekend rates. We are careful where we eat, so we don't spend too much money. We enjoy just walking around and sleeping in late and having a good time.

Another opportunity for utilizing our fun money is taking day trips, particularly on Saturday. We will get up in the morning and decide that we want to visit a place that we haven't been to before. We will get in the car and just drive off. We enjoy visiting historical sights. We moved to Texas a few years ago, so there are a lot of things we don't know about Texas but want to find out. We want to see special geography (hills, lakes, etc.). We go to old towns to see what they are like and look at special monuments. If you have the opportunity, take a train ride with your family to a different city and walk around and visit things that are of interest. You might use a train trip to participate in athletic recreation in another locality, either on your vacation, a weekend excursion, or a daytrip, where you would go water skiing, snow skiing, boating, swimming, hiking, or mountain climbing. Taking a couple of families out to play volleyball together can also be fun.

Satisfaction Is from Relationships

We think that material things are what are going to bring us satisfaction, but what really brings satisfaction is a positive relationship with God, family and friends. We should use our fun money to develop those relationships where we are enjoying things but, in the process, we are getting to know people better, spending time together, and feeling a part of something.

We also use our fun money to buy things that would be exciting as gifts, such as flowers for a spouse when there is no special occasion, or a game for the family to play on a rainy day. Fun money may buy things that your spouse or children looked at and desired but that you didn't have enough cash in the past to buy them. Now you have saved up a little extra to bring that home for them.

We give our kids an allowance for certain chores. We encourage them to save and to learn these same principles. We encourage them to give to God, to save money, and then have money available for spending. Now, when we go to the store and the kids, as all kids do, ask every ten seconds for something to purchase, we just say "Do you have enough money?" If they don't, then they don't get it. They need to learn that, if they want something, they have to save up for it and then get it. If they blow their money, then they don't have any more to spend on things that they want. This has taught them these principles in a very practical way and has relieved us of constant hassle.

In conclusion, for fun money, (1) always use cash, (2) think through which things would be exciting for your family to do (along with other couples sometimes), and (3) use the time for entertainment to build relationships. It is important to spend time together.

There are many things that we can do that are free or of little expense. If you want to take part in a fun activity that is expensive (like certain vacations), then save up for it ahead of time, and don't feel guilty about it. Remember that Christ came so you could have eternal life and serve

Him, but He also came so you could experience an abundant life (John 10:10).

Psychiatric Comment:

The more *obsessive* an individual is the less fun he has. The more *hysterical* an individual is the more fun he has, but it is unfulfilling fun. The more *cyclothymic* an individual is the more he alternates between the extremes mentioned above. Certainly, there is a healthy balance. Let's pray to find that.

CHAPTER ELEVEN
Starting the Diet

Now that you understand all these principles, the big question is, How do you get started? As with any diet, you need to analyze your intake and output.

Prepare a Balance Sheet
(See Appendix A—pg. 117)

So, the first thing you do is prepare a balance sheet and a summary of how much money you spend on a monthly basis.

Proverbs 27:23-27 says that we should look to the state of our flocks, and that the wise man understands what he has. A balance sheet is a listing of the things that you own and the things that you owe. List on a piece of paper the following items: (1) How much cash is in the bank (checking and savings). (2) How much you have in stocks, and notes receivable or accounts receivable that people owe you *and is likely to be collected*. (3) The realistic value of your home *if you had to sell it today*. (4) The resale value of automobiles, personal belongings, furniture, clothing, jewelry, etc. (5) The real value of any investments that you have.

Then, on the liability side, list what you owe. List your credit card bills, loans from the bank, mortgage, any auto loans, and any money that you owe anybody else. Add up those two columns and see if you own more than you owe. If you owe more than you own, it would be prudent for you to go see an attorney immediately and see what options you have to get yourself out of bankruptcy, because you are truly in financial bondage.

Develop an Income and Expense Summary
(See Appendix A—pg. 116)

Once you understand what you have, develop a summary of how much money you are spending. The best way to do that is to make a category heading of the following: housing, automobile, taxes, insurances, loans, food, entertainment, clothing, children, utilities, gifts, tithing, miscellaneous. Go through your checkbook for the last four months and write down each check that you have written into one of the categories. If you have written checks out to cash and don't know where the cash went, put it under miscellaneous. Perhaps you will see that you have a large miscellaneous expenditure.

Establish Your Budget

The key to getting on the diet, now that you understand how much you have and how much you are spending, is to do the following:

(1) Pray for help. Ask God to give you the strength and courage to discipline yourself. Ask Him to bless you so that you might get out of financial bondage, which is His desire as well.

(2) Ask someone else to help you. Possibly, ask someone who is an expert, but definitely someone who, in working with you and your spouse, would be more objective than you are. Go over the balance sheet and the spending statement and let him or her help you decide how best to prepare your plan.

(3) Evaluate all your expenditures in the three areas that were presented previously: (a) those things you *must* have, (b) those things you *should* have, and (c) those things you would *like* to have. The total of the three categories equals the *total* of your spending. Perhaps you will see at the end of each month how much money you have in the "shoulds" and "wants" as opposed to the "must haves." Perhaps it will give you an indication of where you are in trouble. By the way, if your "must haves" are large, and you are still in financial trouble, it is probably because you are in too large a house or have too big a car payment. You may need to consider selling your house and scaling down your living to get it in line with your income.

(4) Work out a plan to cut down your living expenses to the minimum by reviewing each item, cutting out the "would like to haves," boiling down the "should haves," and maybe having it end up with the "must haves." The key is to cut out things until you are in balance with your income. Remember to put the priorities of placing God first and yourself second. If you have never put giving to the Lord in your budget before, you need to add that. You may need to cut back more of your spending to do so.

(5) Under no circumstances should you add any more debt. Please don't get caught in the trap of thinking "Well, I'll take care of all these loans by getting a consolidation loan." You will only wind up paying more interest and will never end up getting your balances paid down. Don't go

borrow more and don't go consolidate your loans. Let the Lord take care of that.

Once you have done this, then develop a budget for your future spending for the next twelve months. Don't buy any "like to have's" until you have saved up enough to pay *cash* for them. This establishes your priorities of purchasing. Don't forget to allow for those major payments that don't normally occur in an average month, such as: insurance payments, quarterly tax payments, real estate taxes, etc. You may also want to put in special purchase items, such as clothes for the kids in the summer and Christmas presents in the late fall or early winter. Another item you need to look at would be gifts for birthdays, anniversaries, etc. In our own family, between June 1 and July 15 we have six birthdays and anniversaries. That is a heavy gift time for us, so we know ahead of time to save up for it.

Add up your budget and make sure that the monthly expenditure is less than your monthly net income. If it exceeds it in any particular month, then you need to pull back your "should have's" so that they come in line. You also need to leave a contingency factor for unexpected events like automobile repair.

Once you have established your budget, you and your spouse need to review this with your counselor or "objective" friend. Then establish that budget as rules and guidelines for the whole family, so that expectations are not unreasonable and it doesn't produce conflict as the spending takes place throughout the year. As you discuss expectations, your frustration level will reduce significantly. My wife and I continually work at agreeing on our priorities on purchasing and our budget for the upcoming months, so that we understand where we will be spending our money. This also gives the perspective of time and we see that, if we save on a regular basis for certain items that we wish to purchase, then it is much easier to purchase them. It doesn't take long before we accumulate enough to purchase them, and we relieve ourselves of that financial burden of adding debt to our financial structure.

Decide to Get Going

The most important aspect of starting the diet is to decide to get going. Keep disciplining the priorities that you have established, namely, to give to the Lord first, to save second, to take care of your family needs third, to pay off your debts, and to spend wisely. Make a conscious effort to discipline yourself to stay on this diet. When we start a diet of food, it seems to be easy the first few days and we determine that we are going to do it. But then we begin to fall into our old habits and pretty soon we are off the diet.

Thus, a critical aspect of starting and getting on the money diet would be to establish accountability to another friend or counselor. Successful dieting programs exist where peer pressure comes into effect—where we are accountable to someone else to stay on the diet. So, record the diet, agree to stick to it with your family, and then establish an outside counselor or friend to give you that accountability to keep you on track and to work through the discipline and the hard part when you begin to fall back into your previous patterns.

APPENDIX A

MONTHLY INCOME AND EXPENSE SUMMARY

INCOME

Gross Pay: _____

Less: FICA: _____

Federal Taxes: _____

State Taxes: _____

Net Pay: _____

EXPENSES

Giving: _____

Savings: _____

Rent/Mortgage: _____

Auto Payment: _____

Utilities: _____

Phone: _____

Food: _____

Clothes: _____

Entertainment: _____

Education: _____

Gifts: _____

Cleaning: _____

Credit Card Payments: _____

Loan Payments: _____

Miscellaneous: _____

TOTAL: _____

What Is Left Over: _____

Other Once in a While Expenses I Need to Budget For:

Taxes: _____

Insurance: _____

Other: _____

BALANCE SHEET

ASSETS

Cash: _____

Average Checking
Balance: _____

CD's: _____

Money Market Funds: _____

　　Total Liquid Funds: _____

ACCOUNTS RECEIVABLE
(What People Owe Me)

Stocks: _____

Bonds: _____

Cash Value of
Insurance: _____

Automobiles: _____

Home: _____

Other Real Estate: _____

Investments: _____

Furniture: _____

Clothes: _____

Jewelry: _____

Other: _____

_____

Total Assets: _____

LIABILITIES

Credit Cards: _____

Bank Loans: _____

House Mortgage: _____

Other Loans: _____

NOTES PAYABLE: _____
(What I Owe)
Other: _____

_____

Total Liabilities: _____

Net Worth: _____
(Assets – Liabilities)

Total: _____
(Liabilities + Net Worth)

CHAPTER TWELVE

Staying on and Maintaining the Diet

The critical time for the money diet is that first month or two where temptation will try to move you away from your diet. You go to a sale and you see something that is really a good buy. You will be tempted to pay extra cash for it and get off your diet immediately. Or Satan will try to defeat you when a major problem comes up, like a car repair, or sickness in the family, or an unusual bill that you weren't expecting, or the insurance payment that you forgot about. You will say "Oh, what the heck, it's just not worth it. There is never enough money anyway, so we might as well give up." This frequently happens when we start a regular food diet, too. We don't see results immediately, so we just quit. Thus the key to success is to discipline yourself and to stay on that budget that you have established.

Jesus says that he that is faithful in small things shall be given great things to be responsible for. I believe that it is at this particular point that you can demonstrate your faithfulness in small things. Only you can choose between your desire to quit and do just what you want, or the better path of working through the pain and staying on the diet.

I can remember when I was on vacation in

Portland, Maine. My kids wanted to jog around the block for exercise. I said, "Oh great, I'll go with you." We started to jog around the block and I couldn't even make half the block, because I was so overweight and out of shape. I was thoroughly disgusted, as I had always felt bad about my weight. I said to myself, "I am going to go on a diet, and I am going to exercise, and I am going to get this area under control." Finally, I desired to lose weight enough to get on a diet, because I was so dissatisfied with my state of affairs.

I am sure many of you can relate to that, both with your weight and financial situations. You were disgusted with the way things were going and really wanted to change, so you said, "Yes, I am going to get on a diet. I am going to do this." Then you started. And you were really committed to it for the first day or two, or even the first week or longer. Then it began to fall apart.

I can remember, when I was on a diet, how tempting it was to eat desserts or to have second helpings, when I knew I should have only one. When I started jogging, there was so much pain in my legs that I didn't want to get out of bed, much less go out and jog. I thought I might as well give up, because I would never make it anyway. But for some reason, God gave me extra strength to discipline myself, and I got up despite the pain. Pretty soon, there was less pain and I started losing weight. Within one year I lost fifty pounds and ran in a 26.2 mile marathon. It was exciting to see it happen. After awhile it became easy to stay on the diet and to keep exercising.

Discipline Produces Suffering
Before Freedom

The thing that I learned during that process is that, to stay on a diet, we *must* suffer, and it *is* painful, but the *freedom* that comes after the pain is wonderful!

When Linda and I were going through our period of overcoming debt, we didn't go out on many dates, we didn't go out to dinner, we didn't buy extra things, and it *was* painful, particularly in today's culture. We saw so many people around us having things—bigger houses, better cars, more clothes — while we were going through this period of pain by not spending any money and not enjoying the financial rewards of life. We sometimes wondered if it was worth it.

Now, I can guarantee you that the freedom that comes from working through that pain for a period of time, until you get in financial shape, *is* worth it. It is a decision you *must* make and preferably make before the Lord. If you can stick to the diet and stay disciplined with your spending, you will have *freedom*. And it will bring so much joy to you and relieve such a burden that you will not be able to believe it.

Maintaining the Diet

Once you have worked through your money diet and you have financial freedom, you no longer have any debt, your expenditures are less than your income, and you are beginning to save money every month (even more than you budgeted), you will begin to really enjoy that freedom. Be careful not to let down and go away from the budget and begin to just spend money now that you have it, because pretty soon you can develop sloppy habits and get yourself in trouble again, particularly with that one temptation that you know Satan will bring along. There is always a chance to have a little bit more, to get that special deal, to keep up with the Joneses, and to violate the principles that you have been steadily maintaining. As in a food diet, when you begin to move away from that pattern that you have established and start eating desserts again, pretty soon you start putting the pounds back on. All that work that you went through is worthless.

Keep those principles in front of you and agree to stick to them with your spouse. Don't let the big temptation or the big problem allow you to move off the diet that you have so diligently established. It is also important to monitor your progress and to compare your actual spending with your budget. So, every month, compare your real expenditures with what you plan to spend, and compare in terms of whether or not you are doing better or worse than what you expected.

A good friend of mine, Jim Sundberg, with the Kansas City Royals, is a person who has a very nice income from professional baseball. I was impressed with his budgeting system and that he sticks to it. He compares every month what they spend and what they plan to spend. When they begin to over-spend in an area, they cut back to stay within the budget. Jim truly has financial freedom and is saving and investing for the future, because he knows that his income from baseball will be limited to a few years. I admire his discipline and his ability to compare how he is doing month to month and to stay within his budget figures.

This brings up another good point, which is, one of the partners in a marriage is generally a better bookkeeper. That person, whether it is the man or the wife, ought to keep the books and compare how you are spending each month. As you keep statistics month to month, you will be amazed at how well you will begin to control your spending, because you are realizing where all that money is going month to month.

CHAPTER THIRTEEN

Conclusion

Money dieting is pretty tough! It would be easier to just spiritualize it all and say, "Well, I will just let God take care of me and I will just keep doing what I have been doing." But God doesn't promise to bless us when we are not following His principles. He clearly spells out in Scripture His principles for financial success. He wants each one of His children to have true financial success.

Remember how we defined it. Financial success is financial freedom. Financial freedom is where we are at rest and at peace. We have the freedom not to worry and spend time concerned with financial matters. Rather, we have the freedom to minister to other people, to take care of our families, and to witness for the Lord.

So God wants us to have financial success. How then do we accomplish it? First of all, we admit and recognize that we need it and that we are not following God's principles. Then, we establish discipline in prioritizing our financial matters simply. As stated:

(1) Give to the Lord first. Trust in Him. Have faith that He will carry out the great promises that He gives us relative to giving to Him first.

(2) Save. Establish a regular pattern of putting money away for ourselves.

(3) Take care of your family needs. Make sure that your family's values and basic needs are taken care of and that they are never put in

jeopardy. Don't over borrow on your house and don't make investments where they would force you into bankruptcy and you would have to give up your automobiles and extra things that you have accumulated for your family.

(4) Pay off debt promptly. Move very quickly to getting those loans paid off and having absolutely no debt, as we defined debt, which is where we owe more than we own. We do not use loans for such things as experiences, or depreciating items, with the exception of half the cost of an automobile, as we discussed.

(5) Spend wisely. Shop around, compare, and budget for those things which you wish to purchase, and then pay cash. Use prudence, letting the Lord show you the way to spend so that it doesn't place burdens on you.

Once you establish these priorities, the key is to start the diet, analyzing where you are, developing a budget, and then staying on it, with discipline, over time.

Yes, it will be painful. Yes, it will require suffering, particularly compared to others who are around you. But once you stay on the diet, over a period of time, you will have the freedom that God wants you to have.

Key Principles

We encourage you to review the key principles, evaluate your real situation, and come before the Lord with sincere desire to gain financial freedom.

I. Ask for help.
   A. Pray.
   B. Be responsible; work hard.
   C. Observe the don'ts.
      1. Don't be drastic.
      2. Don't suddenly quit your job.
      3. Don't suddenly change to a commission job.
      4. Don't fall for a get-rich-quick scheme.
      5. Don't borrow to invest.
   D. Look for creative resourcefulness.
   E. Monitor current investments.
   F. Get wise counsel.
   G. Decrease spending.
      1. Must have's.
      2. Should have's.
      3. Like to have's.
   H. Suffer.
   I. Don't incur more debt.
   J. Get the pressure off.
II. Give.
III. Save.
IV. Get out of debt.
V. Take care of the family.
VI. Spend wisely.
VII. Have fun money.